Off The

Rails

A Genetic Genealogy Mystery
Investigation Book Two

Christine Burke

Pony Tale Publishing

CONTENTS

Chapter One

In their small, bustling office, on a regular Tuesday morning, Olivia, a seasoned ex-cop and private eye, sat at her desk, deep in the midst of reviewing case files. Her assistant, Lilly, focused on meticulously organizing DNA results on her computer screen.

Their desks were usually littered with piles of research, cold case files, half-empty coffee cups, and Diet Pepsi cans, each marking a different stage of their day. The incessant hum of computers and the stale scent of coffee were the background tracks to their lives as forensic genetic genealogists. For them, work was a blend of thrilling discoveries and painstaking research, infused with a hearty splash of caffeine.

Their latest project was an adoption case. A young woman named Jennifer had approached Olivia, desperate to find her birth parents. With limited information and a tangled web of legal obstacles, it seemed like an insurmountable task. But Olivia and Lilly thrived on challenges, pouring over adoption records, birth certificates, and especially DNA test results working to reveal the missing puzzle pieces.

As they were digging deeper into Jennifer's case, Olivia's phone rang, disturbing the focused silence of the office. Startled, she reached for the receiver and answered, "Olivia Mason. How can I help you?"

"Olivia, it's Chief Thompson from the Desert Oasis, Nevada Police Department," came the deep voice on the other end of the line.

Olivia was curious. She motioned for Lilly to come closer, knowing that a call from law enforcement usually meant an intriguing case was on the horizon. She put the phone on speaker and said, "Chief, what can I do for you today?"

"We've stumbled upon a case that might be right up your alley," the Chief explained. "We were going through the archives, and we've got a case from 1983. It's been cold for a long time, but we thought genetic genealogy might do the trick. We recovered a partial skeleton of a male in the vicinity of Jackrabbit Mountain, just on the outskirts of Desert Oasis. It appears to have been there a while, and we're hoping you can help us identify the person. It's very intriguing. I know you're very busy, but if you have the time, we'd love to bring you in to help."

Olivia glanced at Lilly, who was nodding and making the thumbs-up sign. This was the type of case they were both drawn to — a mystery waiting to be solved, a life waiting to be remembered.

"Chief, do you have any other details? How was the skeleton found? Are there any things that might help identify him?" Olivia asked.

The Chief paused for a moment, gathering his thoughts. "A group of hikers were out exploring the mountain when they found him. They stumbled upon a shallow grave, partially exposed due to years of erosion. The remains were pretty decomposed, making normal identification methods difficult. However, we think genetic genealogy can give us the answers we need."

Olivia was excited as she valued any opportunity to use her skills in a case to help the police. "We'd be honored to assist you, Chief," she replied. "Jackrabbit Mountain, you said? We'll make our way there as soon as possible."

Chief Thompson thanked her, explaining that the scene had long been cleared but gave Olivia the details and GPS coordinates. As she hung up the phone, she was grateful for the opportunity to cross one more case off the list. Her mission was to help identify the ever-growing 14,400 unknown humans who had died nameless across the United States, and this was one of them.

Once the call ended, Olivia turned to Lilly, a smile on her face.

Lilly let out a low whistle. "1983? That's one frosty cold case."

Olivia nodded. "Yes it is, but I'm sure we can thaw it."

A somber yet charged ripple of excitement seemed to zap through the room. They had a hard time being patient when a new case came along, but first, they had other commitments to consider. Their current caseload demanded attention, and their personal lives weren't exactly empty.

"When were you thinking of going? We're knee-deep in the Richmond estate dispute," Lilly reminded her, pointing to the stack of cases on Olivia's desk. "And weren't you and Captain Hottie supposed to get together this weekend?"

Olivia grinned, her mind already spinning with the logistics. She loved this part - the thrill of a new case, the puzzle waiting to be solved. "I guess we're taking a trip to Desert Oasis right after we finish the Richmond case. And "Hottie" as you call him will certainly understand. Sometimes it's only cops who truly understand the lifestyle."

Besides, if there was one thing Olivia and Lilly lived for, it was solving cold cases. Despite the everyday challenges, they were committed to their craft. And right now, that meant taking a journey back to 1983, to the mountains of Desert Oasis. They were all in.

Olivia sighed as she dialed TJ's number, hoping to hear his soothing voice that always calmed her nerves. When he answered, she said, "Hey there, Captain Hottie. I'm afraid I've got some bad news for you."

TJ chuckled, already knowing what to expect. "Let me guess, another dead body?"

"You're good," Olivia laughed. "It's like you have a sixth sense for this stuff."

"Well, it comes with the job, I suppose," he replied. "So, what's the story this time?"

Olivia filled him in on the details of the new case. TJ listened attentively, always supportive of her work. "Any leads?" he asked.

"Not yet," she admitted. "But we'll figure it out. You know me, I never back down from a challenge. And with genetic genealogy, we have a good shot."

"That's why I fell for you, Liv. Your determination is something else," TJ said warmly.

Olivia's heart swelled with affection. "Thanks, hon. I appreciate the encouragement. How about you? What's happening on your end?"

TJ's voice turned serious. "We've got an officer-involved shooting. It's messy, but everyone is okay."

Relief washed over Olivia, and she smiled. "I'm glad to hear that. You guys take care of yourselves out there, okay?"

"I will. And you make sure to stay safe too. We'll find another time to see each other, just like we always do," TJ assured her.

"For sure," Olivia agreed.

Personal lives postponed and the skeleton from 1983 and the secrets hidden within Jackrabbit Mountain beckoned. But first, the practical matters of travel arrangements needed attention. Lilly pulled out her phone and started searching for flights and rental cars. Olivia peered over her shoulder.

"Alright, let's dive into this trip planning!" Lilly said, tapping away on her phone screen. "Desert Oasis, here we come! So, we've got two flight options - a morning one that lands early afternoon or an evening flight just in time for dinner."

Olivia pondered the choices, weighing their schedule and the urgency of the case. "I think the morning flight is the way to go. That'll give us a head start, and we can hit the ground running."

"Morning flight it is!" Lilly confirmed, making the booking. "Now, onto the wheels. We need something reliable and roomy enough for all our gear."

Olivia scrolled through the rental car options, her eyes lighting up when she spotted a sleek SUV. "Check this one out! It's got enough cargo space for all our stuff, and it'll handle the rugged terrain near Jackrabbit Mountain like a pro. Plus, we'll be cruising in style during our drives."

Lilly let out a playful sigh. "Okay, I guess we'll save the sports car dreams for another time. SUV it is! Now, let's talk shut-eye. We want a hotel that's convenient but not smack on the Strip. We need some peace and quiet after a day of chasing clues."

Olivia recalled their pact to experience the local vibe whenever they traveled. Desert Oasis, so close to the glitz and glamour of Las Vegas, offered a perfect opportunity. "Exactly. Let's find a hotel near the action, but not right in the thick of it. We'll get the best of both worlds."

With enthusiasm, Lilly searched for the ideal hotel, options popping up on her phone. "Here are a couple that fit the bill. One has an amazing view of the city lights, and the other is just steps away from shows and entertainment. What do you think?"

Olivia considered their options, envisioning moments of relaxation and fun amidst their investigative work. "I say we go with the one near the shows. After a day of sifting through dusty archives and hiking around, we'll deserve some entertainment."

Lilly grinned, hitting the button to reserve their hotel. "Done and done! Our adventure is coming together nicely. I can already feel the thrill of solving this mystery."

The excitement in the room was palpable as their plans fell into place. Flights, rental car, and hotel were locked in - they were ready for their journey to Desert Oasis. The promise of unearthing the secrets of Jackrabbit Mountain during the day and indulging in the vibrant cityscape by night was too enticing to resist.

In the days following the call from Desert Oasis PD, the office was a hive of activity. The air buzzed with a mix of urgency, determination, and a dash of organized chaos that came from managing multiple cases. Olivia, Lilly, and the rest of their small but robust team were no strangers to multitasking, but the upcoming trip added a layer of complexity.

Their current high-stakes case was the Richmond estate dispute. It was a tangled mess of distant relatives and questionable wills, the kind of case that demanded patience, precision, and a lot of coffee.

"I've cross-referenced the wills three times, Olivia," Lilly stated, her eyes defeated as she stared at her computer screen. "There's something off about the Aunt, Matilda's, signature."

As usual, all at the same time, several other cases demanded their attention. These were prior mysteries that had been investigated, knots that had been untied, but still required the neat bow of finality - paperwork to complete, reports to finalize, and phone calls to make.

In the office, as usual, the phone seemed to ring constantly, and Olivia adeptly fielded each call. Potential new clients spun tales of family secrets and long-lost relatives, each hopeful that Olivia and her team could provide answers.

One morning, Olivia found herself on the phone with a potential client, a lady claiming her family was related to the British royal family. "I understand your enthusiasm, Mrs. Jenkins," Olivia said, a smirk playing on her lips as she listened to the passionate ramblings about a great-great-great-grandmother who was supposedly a distant cousin of Queen Victoria.

As she reminisced, Olivia's mind couldn't help but wander to the myriad of strange and unusual cases that had crossed her desk over the years. From eccentric claims of alien abductions to finding long-lost treasures buried in suburban backyards; as a cop and a private investigator, Olivia had seen and heard it all.

With a mixture of amusement and a touch of fondness for the peculiarities of her cases, Olivia couldn't help but reflect on the variety that came with being a detective. It was this very unpredictability that kept her passionate about the job.

CHAPTER TWO

The day before their departure, they found themselves in the chaos of a local shopping mall, a mission Olivia claimed was of utmost importance; finding outfits for Desert Oasis, and nearby Sin City. Excited about seeing some shows and getting away from the normal hum drum, they cracked each other up, trying on increasingly outrageous outfits, their laughter a welcome reprieve from the usual seriousness of their profession.

Finally, back at the office, as they gathered their traveling gear and prepared to head out, Olivia couldn't help but feel a tug of responsibility towards both Jennifer's biological family and the unidentified John Doe. No one case was more important; each one a chance to bring closure, and to provide comfort to those whose lives had been touched by mystery and loss.

As they closed their laptops, Olivia turned to Lilly with a smile. "You know our intern, Victoria? She's been doing fantastic in her practical exercises. I think it's time to give her a taste of the real deal. While we're out of town, I'll have her temporarily join Jennifer's case. She can keep the research going and provide us with updates to review. That way, Jennifer's search keeps moving forward, even while we're away."

Lilly's eyes lit up with agreement. "That's a brilliant plan. Victoria's got the skills, and she'll handle the day-to-day like a pro. We'll stay connected and make sure Jennifer knows we're fully dedicated to her case, even from a distance."

Olivia chuckled, appreciating Lilly's understanding of her thoughtful nature. "You know me so well, Lilly. I couldn't leave Jennifer hanging. Now, let's lock up the office and get ready for the mystery that awaits us on Jackrabbit Mountain."

With a sense of excitement and purpose, Olivia and Lilly secured the office, knowing they had an ace up their sleeve with Victoria's assistance. The journey to Desert Oasis promised not only a challenging case to unravel but also an opportunity to nurture a budding investigator's talents. As they stepped out into the world, they were ready to embrace the thrill of uncovering secrets, and they couldn't wait to see how the pieces of the puzzle would fall into place.

Arriving at the airport the next morning, Olivia and Lilly checked in their luggage and made their way to the gate area. Olivia wore a jacket embroidered with their agency's logo, sparking the curiosity of a fellow traveler.

As they settled into their seats, a friendly stranger, a middle-aged man with a warm smile, approached. "Excuse me, I couldn't help but notice your jacket. Do you two do DNA investigations?"

Olivia nodded, returning his smile. "You bet! We're private investigators specializing in genetic genealogy. It's like being detectives with a scientific twist. We use DNA analysis and genealogical research to crack cold cases and uncover family connections."

The stranger's eyes lit up with intrigue. "Wow, that sounds absolutely fascinating! I've never heard of anything like it before."

Lilly chimed in, eager to share their passion. "It's quite the journey! Our work is a blend of science, history, and puzzle-solving. We help bring closure to families and untangle mysteries that have stumped people for years."

Curiosity getting the better of him, the stranger leaned in. "Tell me, have you come across any cases that have really left a lasting impression on you?"

Olivia took a moment to reflect, her eyes filled with memories of the cases they've tackled. "Oh, there are so many remarkable stories. One that stands out involved a man missing for over two decades. It was a heartbreaking discovery that he had passed away, but we were able to trace his biological family. The closure we provided meant the world to them, finally knowing what happened to their loved one and being able to give him a proper farewell."

The stranger nodded, touched by the emotional aspect of their work. "It must be incredibly rewarding to make such a difference in people's lives."

Lilly's face glowed with genuine warmth. "Absolutely! That's what keeps us going every day. Knowing that we can bring comfort and answers to those who have been searching for so long, it's a privilege."

The stranger extended his hand with admiration. "Well, I commend you both for your dedication and unique skills. It's been a pleasure chatting with you."

Olivia and Lilly shook his hand, grateful for the genuine connection they had made. "Thank you so much! We love what we do, and it's always nice to meet someone who appreciates it."

As the stranger bid them farewell, Olivia and Lilly exchanged knowing glances. The conversation reminded them of the profound impact their work had on people's lives. The mystery of Jackrabbit Mountain awaited them, but they knew that their real-life encounters and the connections they made along the way were what made their journey as investigators truly extraordinary.

Just then, an announcement came over the loudspeaker, signaling their flight boarding. Olivia and Lilly bid farewell to the stranger, their conversation lingering in their thoughts as they made their way onto the plane.

Settling into their seats, Olivia turned to Lilly. "It's always fun to share our work with others. You never know who you might inspire."

Lilly nodded. "So true. Our work has the power to touch lives, even beyond the cases we directly work on. Like a ripple effect, I think."

As the plane taxied down the runway, Olivia and Lilly sat back, getting comfy in their seats, thinking of the adventure that lay ahead. Desert Oasis, Jackrabbit Mountain, and giving John Doe his identity again.

After what felt like a day's worth of flying, Olivia and Lilly finally touched down in Las Vegas, the desert heat instantly embracing them as they stepped onto the jet bridge. The scorching sun seemed determined to test their detective skills, but Olivia saw it as a challenge. "Well, Lilly, if we can solve mysteries in this heat, we can do it anywhere!"

Lilly chuckled, wiping a bead of sweat from her forehead. "You're right. It's like having a natural magnifying glass with this sun."

They swiftly navigated through the bustling terminal, a well-practiced routine from their many investigations. At the car rental agency, Olivia insisted on a dependable SUV instead of the tempting offer of a flashy red convertible. Lilly playfully sighed, knowing better than to argue.

With GPS coordinates from Chief Thompson in hand, they headed north on the highway, leaving the glitz of Las Vegas behind for the rugged beauty of the desert. The landscape transformed, and as Jackrabbit Mountain loomed in the distance, Olivia's excitement grew. "Can you believe it, Lilly? We're heading to the very spot where it all began. The place where John Doe was found. I can't wait to uncover the secrets hidden in these hills."

Lilly nodded, sharing her enthusiasm. "It's always thrilling to step back in time, to imagine what happened all those years ago. The mystery never gets old."

Finally arriving at the entrance to Jackrabbit Mountain, they stepped out of the SUV onto the dusty ground. The desert silence surrounded them as they approached the cave where the partial skeleton was discovered. The wind whispered through the hills, adding an eerie touch to the scene.

Olivia glanced at the cave's entrance, a mix of anticipation and determination in her eyes. "Let's get in there, gather any evidence we can, and start piecing it all together."

With flashlights in hand, they cautiously explored the cave, keen to uncover any overlooked clues from years ago. The air inside felt cool and musty as if it held the secrets of the past.

As they carefully documented everything they found, Lilly placed a reassuring hand on Olivia's shoulder. "We're doing everything we can to help him, Olivia. We'll get the answers we need."

Olivia nodded, grateful for Lilly's support. "You're right. Let's finish up here, regroup, and then we'll touch base with Chief Thompson. Our investigation is just getting started."

Back at the rental car, Olivia eagerly dialed Chief Thompson's number, excited to update him on their progress and discuss the next steps in unraveling the secrets of Jackrabbit Mountain. The journey had officially begun, and both Olivia and Lilly were ready to face whatever twists and turns lay ahead in this captivating mystery.

After a few rings, Chief Thompson's warm voice came through the line. "Olivia, how's everything going? Have you and Lilly arrived at Jackrabbit Mountain?"

Olivia's smile was evident in her response. "We touched down about an hour ago and wasted no time checking out the area. We even explored the cave where John Doe was found. It's an incredible place, Chief—beautiful yet sobering."

The Chief's approval was evident as he replied, "That's great to hear. I knew I could count on you two to jump right into the investigation. How about we meet tomorrow morning at the station? I've already pulled the case file, and we can go through all the details together."

Olivia exchanged a glance with Lilly, who nodded in agreement. "That sounds perfect, Chief. We'll be ready and raring to go. Can't wait to dive deeper into this mystery."

A chuckle came from the other end of the line. "Your enthusiasm is contagious, Olivia. Rest up and get some sleep. Tomorrow will be a busy day."

After thanking the Chief, Olivia ended the call. The lights of Desert Oasis and the glimmering Vegas strip beckoned in the distance as they drove towards their hotel. Their minds buzzed with possibilities, theories, and speculations about the case that awaited them.

As they checked in and settled into their shared room, the excitement in the air was palpable. Olivia couldn't help but feel a mix of exhaustion and exhilaration. "We've already accomplished so much today. Tomorrow, armed with the case file and Chief Thompson's guidance, we'll go even deeper into this investigation."

Ever the organized thinker, Lilly suggested, "Let's take some time now to review all the information we've gathered so far, gather our thoughts, and strategize for tomorrow's meeting."

They spent a half hour going over their notes, discussing ideas, and solidifying their approach. Finally, with their minds buzzing with the unsolved mystery before them, Olivia and Lilly settled into their respective beds, filled with anticipation and determination. As they drifted off to sleep, the echo of the partial skeleton's story filled their minds, and they knew that they were on the path to bringing closure to a decades-old enigma.

CHAPTER THREE

The next morning, Olivia and Lilly found themselves wide awake, their bodies adjusting to the time change. Eager to start the day on a delicious note, they decided to head to the famous Las Vegas Strip for breakfast before heading to the police department. The Paris hotel, with its replica of the Eiffel Tower and charming French touch, beckoned to them.

As they approached the hotel, the architecture caught their attention. The Eiffel Tower replica stood tall against the blue sky, enveloping the surroundings with the charm of Paris.

Olivia noticed a quaint café nestled within the Parisian-themed setting. "Let's have breakfast here."

Lilly eagerly nodded, her stomach growling in agreement. They entered the café, instantly transported to the streets of Paris. The cozy seating, complete with wrought-iron tables and chairs, added to the ambiance.

Indulging in their breakfast, Olivia and Lilly couldn't help but reflect on their surroundings. They chatted about their favorite French movies and actors and daydreamed about faraway places.

After bidding farewell to the charming café, they got their SUV and made their way to Desert Oasis, where the police headquarters awaited them.

Arriving at the imposing building, Olivia and Lilly were greeted by a bustling atmosphere of dedicated law enforcement professionals. After filling out some forms and waiting for a bit, they were escorted into Chief Thompson's office, surrounded by stacks of files and bags of evidence.

"Olivia, Lilly, glad to see you," Chief Thompson warmly greeted them. "Please, have a seat. We have a lot to discuss."

Olivia and Lilly settled into chairs across the Chief's desk, ready to review the case details. Chief Thompson handed them a copy of the case file, filled with reports, photographs, and notes.

"The partial skeleton was discovered on September 1st, 1983," Chief Thompson began, his voice conveying authority. "Based on the estimated age and height, we believe the individual to be a male, around 5 foot 8, and between 30 to 50 years of age. Unfortunately, one or more hands and limbs were not recovered, and the head was missing too, which adds to the complexity of identifying the victim."

Olivia nodded, her eyes focused on the evidence spread out before her. "Do we have any leads on the victim's identity? Any potential matches?"

Chief Thompson sighed with a mix of frustration and determination. "We've exhausted all possible local missing persons cases from that time frame. But there are a few details that might help us narrow down our search. Alongside the partial skeleton, we found a small faded canvas suitcase with United States Postal Service clothing, including a Yeager uniform jacket, a dress shirt, size 16.5, bib overalls labeled Big John, and a pair of eyeglasses, reported as 'spectacles.' This suggests a possible connection to the postal service."

Lilly's analytical mind went into action. "And the spectacles with a nearsighted prescription? They might provide another clue."

The Chief nodded, impressed by their attention to detail. "Exactly. We believe this individual wore spectacles with plastic frames and had a nearsighted prescription. It's a unique characteristic that could aid us in identifying him."

Olivia asked, her eyes fixed on the evidence, "And what about the monogram on the postal shirt? 'IFFE,' does that ring any bells?"

Chief Thompson shook his head. "So far, we haven't been able to make any significant connections with that monogram. It's partial, and missing the first letters. It could be a business name or a personal name; we're not sure. It's another piece of the puzzle we need to unravel."

Olivia examined the Big John bib overalls, her brows knitted in curiosity. "Wow, these seem to be very diverse items of clothing, Chief. Postal service clothing, a dress shirt, and now these bib overalls. It's quite a mix."

Chief Thompson nodded, his gaze fixed on the overalls. "Indeed, it is. The overalls were found with the other clothing items near the partial skeleton. Yet, the body was unclothed. They seem out of place, don't they?"

Lilly chimed in, her eyes narrowing with intrigue. "Chief, could it be possible that our unidentified individual had a history of different occupations? Maybe he worked for the postal service at some point, and these bib overalls were from a different job?"

The Chief nodded thoughtfully. "That's a possibility. It would explain the eclectic assortment of clothing. We might be dealing with someone who had a transient lifestyle, taking on various jobs and perhaps even drifting from place to place."

Olivia's mind whirred with possibilities. "Okay, so we need to gather information on the towns and cities near the railway lines. Look for any information that aligns with our timeline and the Doe's possible presence."

Chief Thompson reached for a map, spreading it out on his desk. "I'll get my team to start compiling information on the areas along the railway lines. We'll dig into the archives, search for any records of missing persons that match the Doe's description."

With a new objective in mind, Olivia, Lilly, and Chief Thompson continued their work on the investigation. The myriad types of clothing became a symbol of the Doe's potential transient lifestyle and the journey they were about to embark upon—an odyssey that would take them through time, space, and the human psyche, revealing the Doe's past one clue at a time.

Hours passed as they studied the intricacies of the case, their conversation a whirlwind of ideas and possibilities. The Chief's team joined in, offering their expertise and insights, adding another layer to the collaborative effort.

At times, the atmosphere in the room grew tense as they faced dead ends and unanswered questions as each offered their own potential plot for the story. Finally, as the afternoon sun cast long shadows across the room, Olivia got up from her chair, a tired but determined glint in her eyes. "Chief Thompson, we've made progress today. We have a clearer understanding of the evidence and potential avenues to explore. But we still have a lot of work to do."

The Chief nodded, his confidence in Olivia and Lilly evident. "Keep following the leads, dig deeper, and we'll support you every step of the way."

Olivia and Lilly left the building, got in the SUV, and found themselves hungry and ready to unwind. They decided to venture out for a well-deserved dinner.

Lilly spotted a charming Italian bistro tucked away in a shopping center not far from the PD. Its inviting ambiance and the aroma of freshly baked bread drew them in. They entered the restaurant and were greeted by the warmth of the cozy interior.

They placed their orders, selecting a variety of dishes that showcased the rich flavors of Italian cuisine. As they waited for their meal to arrive, Olivia leaned back, a contented sigh escaping her lips. "Oh, it's nice to not go, go, go, for a few minutes."

Unable to avoid the case, their conversation turned to the towns and cities the Doe may have visited, the potential crimes left in his wake, and the significance of each clue they had gathered so far. The air buzzed with possibility.

Olivia twirled her fork in her pasta. "I can't help but wonder about those bib overalls found with the victim's belongings. It's such an interesting piece of the puzzle. Who wears overalls for an occupation, especially back in 1983?"

Lilly took a sip of her wine, contemplating the question. "Gosh, I don't really know. Overalls were commonly associated with certain professions, like farmers or construction workers. But it's unusual to find them alongside a postal worker's uniform. It adds another layer of mystery to the case."

Olivia nodded. "It's almost as if our victim had a dual life or some hidden connection that we're yet to uncover. Perhaps he worked in a mail room or had a job that required physical labor alongside his postal duties. Or maybe he had a hobby or side project that involved manual labor."

Lilly tapped her finger on the rim of her wine glass, deep in thought. "You know, it's also worth considering the time period. In the early '80s, there might have been cultural or regional factors at play. Overalls could have been more common in certain areas or industries. We need to dig deeper into the context of that time period and location."

Olivia smiled, impressed by Lilly's insightful analysis. "I agree. Let's look into the history of the area surrounding Jackrabbit Mountain in 1983. Maybe we'll uncover some clues about local industries, trades, or even fashion trends that could shed light on the presence of those bib overalls."

As they enjoyed their desserts, Olivia couldn't help but feel a profound gratitude for the moments like these—the moments of respite amidst the intensity of their investigation. She raised her glass, a toast to their journey and the mysteries yet to be unraveled.

"To the Doe, the unknown victim, and the stories waiting to be told," Olivia said.

Lilly clinked her glass against Olivia's. "To the truth, the justice we seek, and the lives we aim to honor."

After finishing their meal, Olivia and Lilly left the Italian bistro. The night was still young, and the allure of Las Vegas beckoned. They found themselves strolling along the bustling Fremont Street Experience at night, with the dazzling lights and the vibrant energy of Las Vegas surrounding them.

The neon signs illuminated their path, casting a surreal glow on the lively crowd that filled the street. Laughter, music, and the clinking of glasses filled the air, creating a symphony of excitement that echoed through the night.

Olivia breathed in the electrifying atmosphere, feeling the weight of the investigation slowly lift off her shoulders.

"This place is something else, isn't it?" she said to Lilly, her voice filled with awe.

Lilly nodded, her eyes taking in the myriad of sights around them. "It's like a whole different world out here at night. I can see why they call it the 'Fremont Street Experience;' Emphasis on Experience."

As they walked, they found themselves drawn to the street performers, magicians, and musicians who adorned the sidewalks. The sound of a saxophone filled the air, complemented by the tapping of a street dancer's feet. Olivia and Lilly couldn't help but stop for a moment to appreciate the impromptu performance.

"Look at that," Olivia remarked, pointing towards the dancer. "The talent and passion in their art—it's incredible."

Lilly smiled, "It's a reminder that amidst all the bad that we see, there's so much beauty and talent in the world. Moments like these make you appreciate life even more."

They continued their leisurely walk, passing by numerous souvenir shops, restaurants, and quirky attractions that Las Vegas was known for. The famous neon cowboy sign greeted them, known as 'Vegas Vic' an iconic symbol of the city's history.

As they made their way through the crowd, Olivia noticed a small vintage store with old postcards and memorabilia. She pointed towards it, "Let's check that out. Who knows, we might find something interesting to add to our investigation."

Lilly grinned, "I like your spirit. Let's do it!"

In the store, they browsed through the eclectic collection of postcards and historical artifacts. Olivia couldn't help but think of the old letters they sometimes review in their cases. "You know," she said, "there's something magical about handwritten letters. Each one tells a story and leaves a piece of history behind."

Lilly nodded, flipping through a stack of vintage postcards. "It's true. People used to take the time to pen their thoughts and emotions."

"Speaking of time..." Said Olivia, "We are on the losing end of a good night's sleep, so I think we should call it a night and live to explore another day."

"No argument from me," Lilly added, and the two found their car, made their way back to the hotel, and set their sights on a good night's sleep.

The investigation had only just begun, and the mysteries waiting to be unraveled were as vast and intriguing as the city they found themselves in. But for now, they needed rest to recharge their minds and bodies for the journey ahead. Tomorrow would be another day of chasing leads, connecting dots, and following the trail left behind by the enigmatic Doe.

Olivia and Lilly drifted off to sleep, knowing that they were on the brink of something extraordinary. They had found themselves entwined in a story that would unravel across time, guided by the clues left behind in the most unexpected places. And as they closed their eyes, they couldn't help but wonder what other secrets the dawn would reveal.

CHAPTER FOUR

The morning sunlight streamed into the hotel room, casting a warm glow over the table where Olivia and Lilly sat, ready to kickstart their investigation for the day. The first order of business was to send off the DNA samples to the lab for genetic genealogy matching—a pivotal step that might finally lead them to the identity of the Doe.

Sipping her coffee, Lilly appeared deep in thought. "This is where the real magic happens. Once we submit the DNA for testing, we might finally get a lead on the Doe's identity."

Olivia nodded, a mix of excitement and nerves bubbling inside her. "Absolutely. Genetic genealogy has opened up new doors in solving mysteries like this. We'll work to identify the Doe's family and, hopefully, trace it back to him."

Lilly's gaze drifted to the ceiling. "I can't help but wonder who this man was, what led him to Jackrabbit Mountain, and why he met such a tragic fate. I feel like the answers are just within our reach."

Olivia offered a grateful smile. "You're right. We've come a long way, and it's incredible how much we can uncover with the right tools. You, me, and GG—we make a formidable team. There's no mystery we can't solve."

While Lilly pondered what to focus on first, Olivia took charge of ensuring the DNA evidence was properly sent out.

Olivia found herself in the sterile surroundings of the Medical Examiner's office. It wasn't the most glamorous place to be, but it was essential for their investigation. Dr. Peterson, the lead forensic pathologist, greeted her with a warm smile.

"Hey, Dr. Peterson, I'm really grateful for the opportunity to be a part of this process," Olivia said, feeling a mix of excitement and nerves. "This DNA extraction is a crucial piece of the puzzle for our genetic genealogy investigation."

Dr. Peterson nodded, his expression serious yet understanding. "Absolutely, Olivia. We understand the importance of your work, and we've taken all necessary precautions to handle the samples with care. The biological extraction went smoothly, and now we're prepping the samples to be sent off for analysis."

Olivia's eyes lit up with enthusiasm. "That's incredible news, Dr. Peterson! Once we have the results, we can cross-reference the genetic information with commercial DNA databases to identify the victim and even trace his family connections."

Dr. Peterson chuckled softly. "You and Lilly make quite the detective duo. I have no doubt that the DNA testing will yield valuable results. We'll do our best to expedite the process and get you the information as soon as possible."

Leaving the Medical Examiner's office, Olivia felt a renewed sense of determination. She wasted no time and immediately contacted the DNA testing lab, emphasizing the urgency of the case and providing all the necessary details for the incoming shipment.

As she walked back to the hotel, her mind raced with anticipation. She couldn't wait to share the news with Lilly and dive into the next phase of their investigation. Their cozy little mystery was unfolding, and Olivia knew they were getting closer to cracking the case.

Back in the hotel room, Olivia's excitement bubbled over as she shared the good news with Lilly. "You won't believe it, Lilly! Dr. Peterson was thrilled with the DNA samples, and they're already on their way for analysis. We're getting closer to putting a name to Mr. Doe!"

Lilly glanced up from the reports she was studying, her mind still engrossed in the details of the case. "That's fantastic, Liv! But, you know, I've been going through the Medical Examiner's report, and something really stands out. The way the body was dismembered seems unusually brutal, almost ritualistic. We might be dealing with a sadistic killer or someone methodical."

Olivia walked over to take a look at the report, her curiosity piqued. "You're right, Lilly. The level of violence here suggests more than just a simple body disposal. It's like there's a deeper motive behind it all. We need to consider this when we're exploring different angles and possible motives."

As they looked deeper into the details, Olivia noticed something peculiar about the hair found on certain parts of the remains. "Look at this, Lilly. The hair was found in specific regions, but not on others. It can't be postmortem hair growth, right? This adds another layer of mystery to the whole situation."

Lilly pondered the idea and proposed a fascinating theory. "What if we combine elements of both human and animal involvement? Jackrabbit Mountain is surrounded by wilderness, making it a haven for wildlife. But it's also close to Las Vegas, a city with a shady history of organized crime. Could these two factors be related?"

Olivia's eyes lit up with intrigue. "I like where you're going with this, Lilly. The missing limbs might be linked to organized crime's violent disposal methods, while the presence of animal scavengers could have contributed to the dismemberment and the absence of certain body parts."

Olivia quickly searched for more information to support their theory. "According to studies, large predators like bears, mountain lions, or coyotes might scavenge on decomposing bodies, focusing on the soft tissue areas like limbs and head, leaving behind the more skeletal parts."

Lilly nodded, connecting the dots. "So, we're looking at a scenario where a sadistic killer or methodical murderer starts the dismemberment, possibly connected to organized crime. Then, animal scavengers are drawn to the scent of decomposition and contribute to the further dismemberment and absence of specific body parts."

"Exactly!" Olivia agreed. "And the involvement of organized crime could also explain their attempt to obstruct the victim's identification. By removing crucial body parts, they might have aimed to throw investigators off track."

With their new theory taking shape, Olivia and Lilly returned to their computers, eager to dig deeper into their investigation. Their cozy mystery was turning into a thrilling puzzle, and they couldn't wait to see where the clues would lead them next.

While it seemed only a few minutes had passed, it actually had been almost two hours. Lilly got up from her chair, stretched, and sighed. "What a nightmare! This combination of factors adds a huge layer of complexity to the case. It suggests that we should consider not only human motives and actions but also the influence of the natural environment and the criminal underworld in our investigation."

Olivia nodded, a bit bleary-eyed herself. "Well, we're going to have to look at all of it, the intertwining threads of organized crime, animal scavenging, and human violence to figure out what possibly happened. Understanding these connections will be crucial in reconstructing the timeline, identifying potential witnesses, and ultimately bringing justice to the victim."

Lilly paused for a moment, her expression thoughtful. "But Liv, it's important to remember that at this stage, we don't have a confirmed cause of death. As such, our investigation is centered around identifying the victim and bringing closure to their story, rather than focusing on a criminal investigation."

Olivia nodded, acknowledging Lilly's point. "You're absolutely right. Without a confirmed cause of death, our primary goal is to uncover his identity, honor the victim's memory, and provide closure to the community. However, we should remain open to any evidence or leads that might lead us closer to understanding the circumstances surrounding his demise."

Lilly let out an exaggerated groan, slumping in her chair. "My brain is fried. I think I'm turning into a digital zombie."

Olivia chuckled. "Don't worry. We'll get through this like we always do. But right now, we need a snack intervention. Stat!"

While Olivia checked her email, Lilly headed downstairs and straight for the snack bar, her eyes scanning the shelves like a seasoned snack connoisseur. She grabbed an armful of chips, chocolate bars, and even a pack of gummy bears for good measure. She felt like a conquering hero.

As she triumphantly returned to the room, her arms laden with an assortment of goodies, she burst through the door shouting, "Fear not! The goodies are here!"

Olivia's eyes widened, her mouth forming an "O" of anticipation.

Lilly carefully arranged the snacks on the table, presenting them like precious treasures. "We have chips, chocolate, gummy bears, and the secret weapon: peanut butter cups!"

Olivia's face lit up. "You've outdone yourself!"

They both dove into the snacks. As crumbs flew and wrappers crinkled, laughter filled the room, temporarily washing away the fatigue of their research marathon.

The starving situation under control, Olivia and Lilly resumed their research, looking deeper into both animal behavior and organized crime history in Desert Oasis and the surrounding area.

Later that day, Olivia and Lilly were thrilled to find some free time with Dr. Hannah Miller, a renowned zoologist specializing in animal behavior and forensic zoology. They had sought out her expertise to gain insights into the scavenging habits of local wildlife around Jackrabbit Mountain.

With warm smiles, Dr. Miller invited the ladies to take a seat in her office. "I must admit, it's not every day I get approached by private investigators working on such an intriguing case. How can I assist you both?"

Olivia took the lead, introducing the case. "Dr. Miller, we're working with the Desert Oasis Police Department on a case involving partial human remains found at Jackrabbit Mountain in '83. We suspect animal scavengers might have played a part in the dismemberment. Could you enlighten us about the local wildlife and their scavenging behaviors?"

Dr. Miller nodded, happy to help. "Of course. The Desert Oasis area is teeming with diverse wildlife due to its desert and mountainous landscapes. You'll find a mix of predators and scavengers, all with unique behaviors."

Lilly's curiosity was piqued, and she asked, "In our investigation, which animals might be potential scavengers in this region?"

Taking a moment to consider, Dr. Miller replied, "Well, bears and mountain lions are known to scavenge when they catch a whiff of decomposition. They usually focus on the softer parts, like limbs and the head, and leave behind the bonier remains."

Olivia followed up, "What about smaller scavengers like coyotes or foxes? Could they have had a role?"

Dr. Miller nodded again. "Absolutely. Coyotes and foxes are opportunistic feeders and won't pass up a free meal. While they might not fully dismember a body like larger predators, they can still play a part in the scavenging process."

Lilly chimed in, "In our case, the specific absence of body parts, like the head and limbs, is striking. Do animal scavengers typically remove those specific parts?"

Considering the question carefully, Dr. Miller explained, "Scavenging behavior can vary, especially based on available food sources. While some removal of certain parts is not unheard of, the extensive dismemberment you're investigating seems more likely tied to human involvement, rather than purely animal scavenging."

Olivia absorbed the information thoughtfully. "That's an essential distinction to consider. We must explore the possibility of human participation in the dismemberment, potentially linked to organized crime or other motives."

Dr. Miller nodded in agreement. "You're absolutely right. It's vital to keep all possibilities open and gather as much evidence as possible to build a comprehensive case."

As they left Dr. Miller's office, the seriousness of their discussion about animal scavenging still hung in the air, but Olivia and Lilly found a way to lighten the mood.

Olivia raised an eyebrow playfully. "Well, that was quite a talk, wasn't it?"

Lilly chuckled softly, "Definitely not the most cheerful topic, but it's necessary for our investigation."

Olivia nodded with a smile. "True, we need to consider all aspects, no matter how... bone-chilling they may be."

Lilly grinned, playing along. "Nice one. Bone-chilling, indeed."

They shared a good-natured laugh, finding humor in the midst of their serious work.

Olivia grinned mischievously. "Well, at least we can say we're keeping our bones intact on this case!"

Lilly playfully nudged her, "Let's make sure it stays that way!"

Olivia and Lilly decided to take a break from their investigation and treat themselves to a spin on the iconic Las Vegas Strip. The night was alive with vibrant lights and the unmistakable energy that only Vegas could offer.

After grabbing a bite, they hopped into the rental car, excited to catch a glimpse of the latest attraction, the MSG

Sphere, which had been making waves for its distinctive appearance.

Cruising down the Strip, Olivia couldn't help but marvel at the city's transformation. "It's incredible how much this place changes every time I come back. It's like stepping into a different world."

Lilly nodded, her eyes drawn to the mesmerizing billboards that lit up the night sky. "You're right. Vegas really knows how to put on a show and keep things exciting."

Olivia playfully teased, "Speaking of shows, just wait until you see the MSG Sphere. You can't miss it—it's a giant eyeball!"

Lilly chuckled, intrigued by the description. "An eyeball on the Strip? That's something you don't see every day."

"Exactly!" Olivia grinned, her excitement building. "It's like something out of a sci-fi movie. Prepare to be amazed!"

As they approached the Sphere, its futuristic design came into view. The massive structure looked like a gleaming, otherworldly eyeball, capturing the attention of everyone around. Its sleek surface reflected the city lights, giving it an ethereal glow.

Lilly's eyes widened in wonder. "Wow, that's impressive! It's both fascinating and a little eerie."

As they drove along the Strip, they noticed people stopping to take pictures and marvel at the striking sight. The Sphere was quickly becoming a new landmark, cementing its place among the city's iconic attractions.

Olivia couldn't resist a playful remark. "Well, it seems even during our investigation, we're being watched over by a giant eye!"

They shared a laugh, finding humor in the situation. The thought of a gigantic eyeball keeping an eye on them in the bustling streets of Las Vegas added a lighthearted twist to their investigative journey.

As they continued their drive, Olivia and Lilly appreciated the opportunity to take in the city's wonders and recharge. The Sphere left a lasting impression, reminding them of the magic and excitement that made Las Vegas truly unique.

CHAPTER FIVE

Olivia and Lilly woke up with a renewed sense of determination, eager to unravel the mysteries surrounding Jackrabbit Mountain and the enigmatic man. After grabbing a quick breakfast from the hotel's breakfast bar, they settled into their room, ready to dive into the day's work.

Their investigation led them on a trail through Las Vegas and Desert Oasis, delving into the area's shady history of organized crime. Olivia paced back and forth in the room, her mind buzzing with questions about the case. To find answers, she knew she had to tap into her contacts, including an old friend at the FBI who specialized in organized crime. Taking a deep breath, she picked up the phone and dialed the familiar number.

After a few rings, a familiar voice greeted her, "Special Agent Williams speaking."

"Agent Williams, it's Olivia Mason," Olivia said warmly. "Long time no talk. I hope you've been doing well."

A pause followed before Agent Williams responded, "Olivia! It's great to hear from you. What can I do for you today?"

Olivia got straight to the point. "I need your expertise on a case I'm working on. We came across a partial skeleton found in Desert Oasis back in '83. We're exploring potential connections with organized crime and trying to understand if there were any mob activities in that area involving dismemberment."

Agent Williams took a moment to process the information. "1983, huh? That was an interesting time for organized crime in Las Vegas, including Desert Oasis. While I can't go into specific details over the phone, I can confirm that there were instances of mob-related violence during that era. Dismemberment, though not commonplace, did happen as a way of sending messages or disposing of bodies."

Olivia absorbed the information quietly. "I see. So, it's possible that the dismemberment we're looking into could be tied to organized crime activities from that time?"

Agent Williams replied thoughtfully, "It's definitely a possibility. The mob had a presence in Desert Oasis and, of course, Las Vegas, and they weren't strangers to using brutal methods. I suggest looking into specific mob families operating in the area during the early '80s and any known associates involved in violent crimes."

Olivia appreciated the guidance. "That's a good starting point. We were already considering organized crime, but this information will help us narrow our focus. We want to leave no stone unturned in our investigation."

Agent Williams offered reassurance, "I have no doubt that you and Lilly will get to the bottom of this. If there's anything else I can do to assist you, don't hesitate to reach out."

Olivia smiled, feeling grateful for the support. "Thank you, Agent Williams. I'll keep you updated on our progress, and if we come across anything that may require the FBI's involvement, I'll be sure to get in touch."

As Olivia hung up the phone, she felt encouraged by the conversation. With Agent Williams' insights and their dedication to the case, she and Lilly were determined to uncover the truth behind the mysterious remains and bring closure to this long-standing enigma.

With this new information, Olivia and Lilly found themselves at the crossroads of human violence and the raw power of nature. The interplay between organized crime and animal scavenging added a complexity that demanded their utmost attention and resourcefulness.

Yet, at this point in the investigation, they realized that the focus on animal scavenging and intentional dismemberment was not yielding any immediate results. With a collective decision, they temporarily set aside those angles and shifted their attention to other aspects of the case.

Olivia spread out a stack of research materials she had gathered the previous night. Maps, historical records, and newspaper clippings sprawled across the table, forming a puzzle of information waiting to be deciphered.

As they researched history of Jackrabbit Mountain, Olivia recalled Chief Thompson's mention of its deep connection to the Union Pacific rail line. In 1983, the area bustled with railway activity, attracting various individuals seeking temporary work or adventure, hopping on and off trains in search of a sense of purpose or a fresh start.

Olivia narrated while peering at the computer screen, piecing together the fragments of information. "It appears that Jackrabbit Mountain was a popular stop for men traveling along the rail line. They must have been drawn by the mountain's allure and the opportunities it offered."

Lilly was engrossed in her own research, scanning articles and photographs online. "It's intriguing how the railroad served as both a lifeline and a pathway to new possibilities. But what led our Doe to Jackrabbit Mountain? Did he willingly choose this place?"

Olivia traced her finger along the railway lines thoughtfully. "It's possible that he was exploring the region, and the mountain's proximity to the rail line made it an appealing destination. However, we can't rule out the idea that he might not have arrived here by choice. We need to keep all scenarios in mind."

Lilly nodded, her mind racing with possibilities. "Exactly. We shouldn't get fixated on just one theory. Jackrabbit Mountain's history offers some insights, but there's still so much we don't know. If he was a drifter, how did he find his way here? Were there any connections he had to the area or its communities? And most importantly, what events unfolded that led to his demise?"

She paused, her thoughts expanding further. "And what if he was a local, simply out for a hike? How is it possible that no one reported him missing?"

Olivia agreed, acknowledging the many unknowns in the case. "Those are precisely the questions we need to find answers to. We have to figure out where to dig for more information."

Olivia spread out a stack of research materials she had gathered the previous night. Maps, historical records, and newspaper clippings sprawled across the table, forming a puzzle of information waiting to be deciphered.

As they viewed the history of Jackrabbit Mountain, Olivia recalled Chief Thompson's mention of its deep connection to the Union Pacific rail line. In 1983, the area bustled with railway activity, attracting various people seeking temporary work or adventure, hopping on and off trains in search of a sense of purpose or a fresh start.

Olivia narrated while peering at the computer screen, piecing together the fragments of information. "It appears that Jackrabbit Mountain was a popular stop for men traveling along the rail line. They must have been drawn by the mountain's allure and the opportunities it offered."

Lilly was engrossed in her own research, scanning articles and photographs online. "It's intriguing how the railroad served as both a lifeline and a pathway to new possibilities. But what led our Doe to Jackrabbit Mountain? Did he willingly choose this place?"

Olivia traced her finger along the railway lines thoughtfully. "It's possible that he was exploring the region, and the mountain's proximity to the rail line made it an appealing destination. However, we can't rule out the idea that he might not have arrived here by choice. We need to keep all scenarios in mind."

Lilly nodded, her mind racing with possibilities. "Exactly. We shouldn't get fixated on just one theory. Jackrabbit Mountain's history offers some insights, but there's still so much we don't know. If he was a drifter, how did he find his way here? Were there any connections he had to the area or its communities? And most importantly, what events unfolded that led to his demise?"

She paused, her thoughts expanding further. "And what if he was a local, simply out for a hike? How is it possible that no one reported him missing?"

Olivia agreed, acknowledging the many unknowns in the case. "Those are precisely the questions we need to find answers to. We have to figure out where to dig for more information."

Intrigued by the history of Jackrabbit Mountain and its connection to the Union Pacific rail line, Olivia and Lilly decided to contact the Union Pacific Railroad Police. They hoped to gain insights into the trains that passed through the area in 1983 and the kinds of cargo they transported.

Olivia picked up her phone, put it on speaker, and dialed the number for the Union Pacific Railroad Police. After a few rings, Officer Johnson answered the call with a friendly and professional tone.

She explained their purpose and asked, "My assistant Lilly and I were wondering if you could provide us with some information about the trains that passed through the area in 1983."

Lilly chimed in, eager to join the conversation. "Yes, we're particularly interested in learning about the types of trains that frequented Jackrabbit Mountain during that time. Any information about the cargo they carried and their origins would be incredibly helpful."

Officer Johnson paused, considering their request. "Well, that's going back some days, but you're in luck. We're actually preparing for the 40-year anniversary celebration, and I was on the research team for that project. From what I recall, Jackrabbit Mountain was a significant stop along our rail line back then. We had a mix of freight trains, intermodal trains, and passenger trains passing through. The cargo they carried varied, depending on the needs of the communities along the route."

Olivia's curiosity was piqued, thinking about overalls. "That's fascinating. Could you give us some more details about the types of goods these trains carried?"

Officer Johnson gladly obliged, "Sure thing. Freight trains were like workhorses, hauling a wide range of commodities such as lumber, coal, oil, manufactured products, and agricultural goods like grains and livestock. These trains played a crucial role in supporting local economies by facilitating trade and supplying essential resources."

Lilly sought further clarification, "And what about intermodal trains? What cargo did they typically transport?"

Officer Johnson explained, "Intermodal trains were the real multitaskers. They carried containers and trailers filled with everything from consumer goods and electronics to machinery and equipment. Their versatility allowed for smooth transfer between trains and trucks, making the transportation of goods efficient across long distances."

Olivia absorbed the information and questioned, "And the passenger trains? Where did they come from, and who were the travelers they served?"

Officer Johnson answered, "Passenger trains were all about connecting people and places. They served both local commuters and long-distance travelers, originating from various parts of the country. Business folks heading to meetings, families embarking on vacations—the passenger trains were the lifeline of mobility."

Recalling the significant cities along the Union Pacific rail line, Johnson added, "The route had several key cities that played crucial roles in the transportation network. For example, Chicago was the 'Windy City' and a major transportation hub where trains from different parts of the country, including the East Coast, Midwest, and Canada, converged. Omaha, Nebraska, was the headquarters of the Union Pacific Railroad, while Salt Lake City, Utah, acted as a major junction connecting the East Coast with the Western states. Denver, Colorado, bridged the gap between the Midwest and the West, and of course, Los Angeles, California, served as a gateway to various destinations, including Desert Oasis."

Olivia thanked Officer Johnson for the valuable information. "Thank you so much. Your knowledge has been incredibly helpful for our investigation."

Johnson replied, "You're welcome. I'm glad I could assist. If you have any more questions or need further help, don't hesitate to reach out. Good luck with your case."

The conversation with Officer Johnson had shed light on the significance of various cities along the Union Pacific rail line. With a clearer understanding of their role in connecting the country, Olivia and Lilly felt invigorated to continue their investigation into Jackrabbit Mountain and John Doe's identity. But before diving back into the case, they needed to check in on intern Victoria and the progress she was making with Jennifer's adoption case.

Eager for a break and some fresh air, Olivia and Lilly decided to sit poolside while waiting for updates. Olivia sat down, cell phone pressed to her ear, soaking up the warm glow of the sun outside. Lilly headed to the to-go window to grab some food.

"Victoria, how's everything going with Jennifer's case?" Olivia inquired, her curiosity piqued.

On the other end of the line, Victoria's voice was filled with enthusiasm, "It's going really well! I downloaded Jennifer's genome from Ancestry.com and uploaded it to FTDNA, GEDmatch, and MyHeritage. We're starting to see some promising matches! While waiting, I've been working on her family tree and have identified a second cousin once removed who could be a significant lead."

Olivia smiled, impressed with Victoria's progress. "You're doing an excellent job. Keep up the great work, and if you hit any roadblocks, don't hesitate to reach out."

"I will.. I've got this," Victoria reassured her. "We'll crack this case wide open, and Jennifer will finally get the answers she's been searching for."

With a satisfied smile, Olivia ended the call, thankful for Victoria's capable assistance. She turned her attention to Lilly, who had returned with a delightful assortment of sandwiches.

"You're a lifesaver! What did you get?" Olivia asked with appreciation.

Lilly proudly unveiled the sandwiches, each one made with fresh ingredients and care. "We've got turkey avocado, roast beef with horseradish, and a classic BLT. Take your pick!"

Olivia took a bite of her food, savoring the flavors before setting her sandwich down, her mind drifting to Lilly's daughter, Rosie.

"Speaking of our genetic work, how is Rosie doing? It's been a year since we found her dad. I hope everything is going well with her new family," Olivia inquired, genuinely concerned.

Lilly's face lit up at the mention of her daughter. She smiled, radiating happiness. "Rosie is thriving. Connecting with her biological father's family has been such a blessing. They welcomed her with open arms, and I couldn't be happier for her. Genetic genealogy has truly changed our lives for the better."

Olivia nodded, touched by Lilly's words. "I'm so glad to hear that, Lilly. It warms my heart to know that our work has brought such happiness to your life and Rosie's. It's a wonderful reminder of the impact we can have on people's lives."

Lilly expressed her gratitude, "I'll forever be thankful to you for helping me find Rosie's father. It was a life-changing moment for both of us. Now, I feel honored to work alongside you, making a difference in other people's lives and reuniting families."

Olivia reached across the table, squeezing Lilly's hand gently. "And I'm grateful to have you by my side, Lilly. Your dedication and passion for genetic genealogy have brought so much value to our work. Together, we make a formidable team, and I know there are countless more lives we'll touch and stories we'll uncover."

As they basked in the laughter and chatter around them, Olivia and Lilly felt a sense of purpose and fulfillment in their shared journey. The impact they had on the lives they touched through their work was a reminder of the importance of their mission and the value of human connection.

Back upstairs, the atmosphere in the hotel room was filled with determination and intrigue as Olivia and Lilly continued their investigation. The train information they had gathered felt like a crucial piece of the puzzle, and they were eager to connect it to John Doe's identity.

Olivia tapped her pen against the table, her mind racing with possibilities. "We need to figure out the significance of that train connection. If we can trace it back to its origin, it might lead us to John Doe's point of origin as well."

Lilly nodded, fully engaged in the task at hand. "Absolutely. But for now, let's focus on the postal uniform. That's something tangible we can work with. I'll start by researching the Yeager Uniform Company and its connection to the US Postal Service."

Olivia grabbed her laptop, her fingers poised to type. "And I'll search for any historical records, news articles, or testimonials related to the company. Maybe we'll find some clues about their clientele or any unusual occurrences."

As Olivia began her online search, Lilly's mind was buzzing with observations. "You know, it's curious that all the clothing items found with John Doe were related to work wear. Overalls, a postal uniform, and a jacket with a faded label. It seems like this person had some kind of occupation or association with these professions."

Olivia agreed, her eyes scanning through the search re-sults. "You're right. These items could be more than just personal belongings—they could be significant clues to John Doe's identity. We should also consider if there were any traveling salespeople for the Yeager Uniform Compa-ny who might have passed through the area around that time."

Lilly scribbled notes in her notebook, her curiosity grow-ing. "And what about the postal uniform? It could mean that our John Doe worked for the US Postal Service or had a connection to someone who did. We should explore any missing persons reports or individuals who had ties to the Postal Service in the area during that period."

Olivia continued to scroll through a webpage, her focus sharp. "Exactly. Let's cross-reference the records and see if any names or incidents match up. We need to cast a wide net and follow every lead, no matter how small."

CHAPTER SIX

While Olivia looked online searching for more information about Yaeger Uniforms and their history of serving the postal community, Lilly flipped through a file of documents, looking for any clues that might link the uniforms to their case.

Olivia spoke up, her eyes scanning the screen. "According to their website, Yaeger Uniforms has been in the postal uniform business since 1956. They claim to be the largest catalog/internet supplier, providing quality apparel to the postal community."

Lilly nodded, taking note of the information. "It's interesting that they emphasize their union/USA-made clothing. This could be a significant clue, as it suggests a potential connection to a specific era or group of employees."

Olivia continued her research, exploring customer reviews and testimonials. "Many customers praise their low prices, fast delivery, and quality products. It seems they offer a range of discounts and services to meet the needs of postal workers."

Lilly chimed in. "I found some details about the USPS-branded shirts. It seems these shirts were specifically designed for postal employees and carried the official USPS logo. They were part of the standard uniform provided by the Postal Service."

Olivia nodded, her eyes shifting to a plain Yaeger jacket mentioned in another document. "On the other hand, it appears that employees could also wear a plain Yaeger jacket as part of their uniform. This might be significant in our investigation, as it could help us differentiate between USPS-branded shirts and potential plain jackets that an employee might wear."

Lilly was making notes. "So, we have two key pieces of information: the USPS-branded shirts and the potential plain Yaeger jacket. We need to determine if the unidentified man found with the bib overalls was a postal worker and whether his uniform included the USPS-branded shirts or the plain jacket."

Olivia agreed. "Right. We'll need to cross-reference any available records, interview former or current postal employees, and reach out to the USPS for more information about their uniform policies during the time frame we're investigating."

Lilly added, "And, we should inquire about any specific markings or identification methods used on the USPS-branded shirts or any other unique features that might help us positively identify the uniform."

Olivia picked up her phone, ready to make a call to Yaeger Uniforms to gather more information about their products and distribution methods. She dialed the customer service number listed on their website, while Lilly continued to sift through the documents, looking for any additional clues.

After a few rings, a friendly voice answered on the other end. "Yaeger Uniforms, how can I assist you?"

"Hello," Olivia began, identifying herself and stating her goal. "I was hoping to gather more information about your products and how someone would obtain them."

The customer service representative, Tricia, responded, "Wow, I don't know what to say. I'll do my best to assist you. Our uniforms are primarily distributed through our catalog and website. We serve a wide range of customers, including the postal community. They can order directly from us, either through their individual accounts or through their respective postal offices. I'm not familiar with what we were doing back then, but I could look into it."

Olivia asked for more specific details. "Are there any restrictions or requirements for individuals to obtain the uniforms? And would it be possible for someone outside of the postal service to acquire them?"

Sarah paused for a moment before responding. "Our primary focus is indeed on serving the postal community, but we do have other customers who purchase our uniforms. While we strive to ensure that our products are primarily available to authorized individuals or organizations, it's difficult to monitor every transaction. However, we rely on our customers to provide accurate information when placing their orders."

Lilly was intrigued by the conversation. "Do you have any specific markings or identification methods on the

USPS branded shirts to differentiate them from other garments?"

Sarah answered. "Yes, the USPS-branded shirts typically include the official USPS logo and may have additional identifiers specific to postal employees. These markers are essential to maintain the integrity of the uniform and to ensure that only authorized individuals are wearing them."

Olivia took notes. "Thank you, Tricia. We'll continue our investigation and may reach out to you again if we have any further questions."

As Olivia ended the call, she turned to Lilly. "It seems that obtaining a Yaeger uniform, including the USPS-branded shirts, requires some level of authorization or association with the postal community. We'll need to dig deeper into the process of obtaining these uniforms and how someone outside of the postal service could potentially get them."

Lilly nodded, her mind already spinning with ideas. "We should also consider interviewing former or current postal employees to gather more information about the distribution methods, any potential loopholes, and if they recall any instances of unauthorized individuals wearing postal uniforms."

Olivia got up and stretched, considering what they had learned. "Specifically, let's look into the difference between the USPS-branded shirts and the potential plain Yaeger jackets. I think that might tell us if John Doe was a Yeager employee or from the Post Office."

Lilly adjusted her glasses, her fingers gliding over the keyboard. "Based on my understanding, the USPS-branded shirts were specifically designed for postal workers. They featured the USPS logo and other relevant insignia. On the other hand, the plain Yaeger jackets might have been worn by employees in government agencies or other industries that required a uniform."

Olivia's mind was continually moving. "That makes sense. It's possible that the Doe possessed a plain Yaeger jacket acquired from a previous job or through other means, rather than directly from the USPS. Okay, so we are still at square one."

Lilly tapped her mouse. "It could be a clue that he had a history of working in a job that required uniforms, but it doesn't necessarily link him directly to the postal service."

Olivia raised an important point. "We shouldn't rule out the possibility that he obtained the uniform from someone else or purchased it second-hand. Uniforms can some-times circulate outside of official channels."

Armed with this new knowledge, Olivia and Lilly con-tinued their research, exploring various channels to gather more information. They scoured online forums, reached out to postal workers' associations, and prepared a list of potential interviews.

The time had come to reach out to the Postal Inspector's Office, hoping to uncover any information about missing post office personnel from 1983 or thereabouts.

Dialing the number, Olivia listened to the rings, her mind drifting back to the history of the Postal Inspector's Office. It was an agency that had been around for over two cen-turies, a silent guardian protecting the integrity of the mail system.

A voice finally answered on the other end, "Postal Inspec-tor's Office, how may I assist you?"

Olivia began, identifying herself and her mission. "I'm hoping to speak with someone who can provide informa-tion about any post office personnel who went missing around 1983. Specifically, we're interested in uncovering any leads related to a John Doe case we're currently investigating."

There was a moment of silence as the person on the other end processed Olivia's request. "One moment, please," came the response, followed by a brief hold.

Olivia grabbed her notepad and pen. The Postal Inspector's Office was known for its thorough investigations, dealing with cases ranging from mail theft to fraud and even employee misconduct. They had the expertise and resources she needed to research the missing personnel records.

A new voice came on the line, authoritative yet cordial. "Special Agent Reynolds."

Olivia felt a surge of confidence, knowing she had reached someone who was in a position to help. She filled him in and pressed forward. "We have reason to believe that a missing post office employee from around 1983 may hold clues to our case. I was wondering if there are any records or information that could help us in our search."

Reynolds listened attentively. "Olivia, we take missing personnel cases seriously. While I can't get into it over the phone, I can assure you that we maintain comprehensive records of employees who went missing or were reported as unaccounted for during that period. We have a team dedicated to investigating such cases, and I'm confident we can assist you in your search."

Olivia's heart raced. This was a promising development, a step closer to uncovering the truth behind the unidentified John Doe. "Wonderful! We would greatly appreciate any assistance you can provide. If there's a process or specific information we need to follow, please let us know, and we'll ensure everything is in order."

Reynold put her mind at ease. "I'll assign one of our investigators to collaborate with your team. We'll gather the necessary details and cross-reference our records to identify any missing post office personnel who might be relevant to your case. We'll keep you informed of any findings and work closely with you to get the answers you need."

A surge of gratitude washed over Olivia. She knew they were on the right path, with the support and expertise of the Postal Inspector's Office at their side. "Thank you. We greatly appreciate your assistance and look forward to working with your team."

With the conversation concluded Olivia hung up the phone. The Postal Inspector's Office had opened its doors, ready to join forces in their pursuit of answers, which was not always the case. Now, it was a matter of patiently waiting for the agent to call, eager to see what discoveries awaited them in the annals of postal history.

Next on the list was the partial monogram on the postal shirt. Olivia and Lilly sat side by side as they examined close-up photos of the embroidered name on the shirt: "...IFFE." It was an unusual combination of letters, and they racked their brains to find any possible surnames that matched.

Lilly was doing her best, squinting at the stitching. "This is quite a challenge. 'IFFE' is an uncommon ending for a surname. We'll need to think outside the box."

Olivia nodded, her eyes scanning the room. "Let's consider different possibilities. Maybe there are unique surnames with this exact ending or ones that are similar in sound but spelled differently. You know very well how names have been translated completely differently between the old world and new world spellings and pronunciation."

They once again turned to their keyboards, searching online databases and exploring genealogy forums, determined to crack the code. As they did their research, they engaged in a lively conversation, bouncing ideas off each other.

One of the first things they did was hit the search engines. They got several responses back including the names Radcliffe, Rafferty, Taffler, Stanscliffe, Ratcliffe, Spofford, Stilcliffe, Shadcliffe, Gaffney, and Heathcliffe.

Olivia huffed in frustration, her fingers furiously tapping on the keyboard. "Stupid machine," she muttered under her breath. "It's giving us names that don't even include the letters we entered."

Lilly let out a sympathetic chuckle. "Well, it seems like technology still has its limitations," she remarked, her eyes scanning the screen. "But don't worry. We'll figure this out with our own detective skills."

Olivia sighed. "I know, I know," she said, a hint of exasperation in her voice. "Sometimes you just can't rely on a machine to do the thinking for you."

"You are so right," Lilly replied. "We'll go back to the old-fashioned way—research, connections, and good old detective work. We won't let a search engine hold us back."

They began pulling up historical records, family trees, and any fragments of information that could provide a glimpse into the lives of those who bore these surnames.

Soon, a pattern emerged. "Radcliffe," Olivia murmured. "It's a name that sounds fancy. Close to Ratcliffe. Could our John Doe have hailed from a line of Radcliffe's?"

"Take a look at this," Olivia exclaimed. "According to the web, the Radcliffe name was big in the USA, the UK, Canada, and Scotland between 1840 and 1920."

Lilly looked over. "It seems like the Radcliffe family had connections in various parts of the world during that time. We should focus on the data from the United States and the United Kingdom, as they had the highest concentrations of Radcliffe families."

Olivia nodded, scrolling through the page. "In 1891, the majority of Radcliffe families were found in the United Kingdom. This fits in with what we know about the Radcliffe surname's origins."

Lilly's eyes widened as she found something. "And did you see this? In 1840, there was one Radcliffe family living in New York. It's a significant lead, especially considering our

John Doe was found in 1983. As a male, he could be a direct descendant."

Olivia kept going. "It's intriguing that Virginia, New York, and South Carolina had the highest population of Radcliffe families in 1840. These states might hold important clues about the Radcliffe family's history and possible connections to our John Doe."

As they continued to sift through the data, Olivia and Lilly felt a sense of excitement building. The geographical information offered valuable clues about the Radcliffe family's presence in specific regions. It was another piece of the puzzle, allowing them to narrow down their focus and investigate further.

"We need to look at the Radcliffe families in New York, Virginia, and South Carolina," Lilly suggested. "There might be local records, census data, or historical archives that can provide additional insights into their lives and any potential ties to our John Doe." We can build trees, look for descendants and see if any of them have migrated out west."

Olivia nodded. "I can start on the Radcliffes."

Lilly's fingers continued to type, moving on to the next names. "Stanscliffe," she announced. "Makes me think of big mountains."

"The Stanscliffe surname appears a lot in these records too," Lilly said. "There are thousands of census records, hundreds of immigration records, and almost a thousand military draft cards. It seems like the Stanscliffe family grew during that time period."

Olivia agreed. "That's a lot for sure. We should focus on the census records to gather more insights into their origins and potential connections."

As they looked into the census records, Olivia and Lilly traced the Stanscliffe families across different states, piecing together their migration patterns and family relationships. The records provided glimpses into their occupations, ages, and household structures, painting a picture of the Stanscliffe family's lives during those times.

"At this point, while we are not able to confirm specific people who directly relate to our John Doe, the abundance of records indicates a large Stanscliffe family history," Lilly remarked. "It's amazing how much information we can gather from these records and how they might contribute to our investigation."

"Even if we don't find an immediate connection, these records might hold valuable clues or point us in the direction of other family branches," Olivia added.

Lilly did not give up but instead continued to review records available online, this time focusing on the surname Heathcliffe. However, she quickly noticed a peculiar trend—the surname seemed to be commonly spelled as Heathcliff, without the final "e."

"It's interesting," Lilly remarked. "While we were expecting records for Heathcliffe, it appears that the surname is normally spelled as H-e-a-t-h-c-l-i-f-f. It seems that the 'e' at the end is often omitted. Without the 'e' on the end, it doesn't match our monogram."

Olivia exhaled a frustrated sigh. "Bummer, but you know how these records are. It could be just bad handwriting or record scanning issues. Let's focus on the records under the Heathcliff spelling and see if we can uncover any potential leads or connections or where the 'e' may have come in or out. I'm pretty sure that someone would want their name spelled correctly on their uniform, right?"

They continued to work for a few more hours and with nothing of significance showing up, decided to call it a day. While the surnames were important to confirm relationships for the Doe, without the DNA they had nothing to start with. They did, though, have some dreams to get after, and they did.

CHAPTER SEVEN

The next morning, Olivia stretched her limbs and let out a contented sigh as she woke up, the anticipation of the day starting to gather. Glancing at the clock, she realized it was time to shake it off and get to work.

"Lilly, rise and shine!" Olivia exclaimed cheerfully. "It's time to grab some breakfast and investigate some overalls."

Olivia threw back the covers, leaped out of bed, and hopped in the shower. She was ready quickly and while waiting for Lilly, she grabbed her phone and searched for a quirky breakfast spot in Las Vegas.

"I've found the perfect place!" Olivia exclaimed. "It's called 'The Eggcentric Café.'

"Eggs, you say? Count me in!" Lilly replied as she finished putting on her shoes.

Olivia grabbed her bag and keys, and they headed out. Traffic was sparse in the early morning hours and it was a relief to be able to take in the sights with a peaceful drive to the restaurant. There, they ate, read the newspaper, and perused social media. They talked about anything but the case and it was a nice break.

As they were headed back to the hotel, Olivia received a call from the lab. The voice on the other end of the line relayed the much-anticipated news. We've completed the initial analysis of the DNA samples. The quality is excellent, and we've successfully extracted a complete genetic profile. You should see results within the next 24 – 48 hours."

Olivia couldn't contain her enthusiasm. "Thank you so much!"

Olivia hung up the phone. She knew that the genetic data held the key to unlocking the secrets surrounding the unidentified man found on Jackrabbit Mountain. But, in the meantime, there were still the old-fashioned investigative methods.

Back at the hotel, as they entered their temporary office in their room, Olivia leaned against the table, her voice softening. "You know, we've gotten a lot done here in Las Vegas," she stated, her tone reflective. "But I can't help but think that it's time to head back home. We've made progress, but we can continue our research remotely."

Lilly nodded, her gaze meeting Olivia's. "As much as I love the thrill of being on the ground, we have other cases that need our attention, and we can continue working on this one from a distance."

The best at finding quick, affordable deals, Lilly went right to work her fingers flying across the keyboard as she searched for the best options. "I'll check for early morning flights that can get us back home without too many layovers," she replied.

With flights booked and confirmation emails in hand, Olivia stretched in her chair, a satisfied smile on her face. "Well, it looks like we're heading back home tomorrow," she said, her voice tinged with a mix of contentment and anticipation.

"We've made great progress, and we can continue our work from our own turf," Lilly replied. But, we still have the day, and we have a lot to learn about those overalls.

She went right to work and soon had her eyes glued to the computer screen displaying information about the Big John bib overall company. Olivia sat beside her, equally engrossed in the fascinating history of the brand.

"Can you believe it?" Lilly asked. "The Big John Brand has been around since 1916! It all started with the Johnson family in Carthage, Missouri. They had a vision to produce and sell high-quality overalls, and boy, did they succeed."

Olivia smiled. "It's incredible how they began on such a small scale and quickly expanded throughout the state."

Lilly scrolled through the timeline of ownership changes. "But their journey hasn't been without ups and downs," she remarked. "In 1971, the Johnson family sold the company, and it went through various changes and challenges over the next few decades. It even faced bankruptcy in 1982."

Olivia scanned the screen. "Yet, just like their overalls, the Big John brand bounced back," she noted. "In 2000, Toms, a renowned workwear brand, acquired them. Toms had a solid reputation for providing tough gear, particularly for workers in the oil industry."

Lilly added, "And the evolution didn't stop there. In 2013, Andy's, another prominent workwear manufacturer, acquired them, creating a powerhouse in the industry," she added, her voice filled with awe. "Now, Big John overalls are part of the Andy's family, the largest workwear manufacturer in the world. Who knew?"

Olivia was surprised that plain old overalls were so impressive. "It's amazing how Big John overalls have stood the test of time. They offer a range of designs, from the classic denim to the stone-washed denim and the striped overall, I had no idea," she explained, her voice filled with admiration.

Lilly couldn't help but imagine the stories behind each well-worn pair of Big John overalls. "You know, it's no wonder that people hold onto their Big John overalls for years. Just like a good pair of jeans. They become a part of their own personal history, just like the brand itself," she mused.

"But wait a minute, think about it." Lilly started. "Big John faced bankruptcy in 1982 and ultimately shut down. Our John Doe was found in 1983, with a pair of Big John overalls. How does that add up?"

Olivia shook her head, contemplating the puzzle before them. "I don't know but it's a good point. It raises questions about how he obtained the overalls. Did he purchase them before the company's closure, or was he somehow connected to Big John brand? Maybe he was an employee, or he had a friend who worked there?"

Lilly wasn't sure. "If he was an employee, it could provide a vital link to his identity. We need to check the timeline, explore the circumstances surrounding Big John's bankruptcy, and determine if any former employees might have gone missing or had connections to our John Doe."

Olivia made a note. "Let's gather as much information as we can about Big John's closure, search for records of former employees, and cross-reference it with our existing findings," she suggested.

As they brainstormed other ideas and strategized their next steps, the room filled with an air of possibilities. The uncertainty surrounding the Big John bib overalls, the Yeager jacket, and their correlation to the unidentified man sparked their curiosity, as well as the possible postal connection, propelling them deeper into their investigation.

Oliva's phone rang. The female identified herself as Agent Beck from the Postal Inspector's Office.

"Agent Beck, thank you for following up," Olivia greeted her. "Were you able to find anything on a potential missing postal employee?"

Agent Beck had a pleasant voice and was very friend-ly. "Good to speak with you. Please, call me Luane. I've checked our database as Special Agent Reynolds asked, and I can confirm that we don't have any reports of missing postal employees from that specific time period. There have been no indications of foul play or disappearances."

Olivia's shoulders slumped slightly, a mixture of disap-pointment and determination swirling within her. "Okay. Hey, I forgot to mention earlier that we have a partial monogram on one of the postal uniforms. It's pretty dis-tinctive, the last four letters '...iffe.' Would you be able to see if you had any employees during that time that might have been working in Nevada that might fit the bill? I can't imagine too many last names with those letters. We actually did a Google search and only came up with a few. Hang on a sec and let me grab them for you."

Agent Beck was reassuring. "Of course. I'll do what I can."

Olivia read Beck the last names from their research and Beck told her she would be in touch.

As they ended the call, Olivia couldn't help but feel a twinge of frustration. The search for clues seemed to be hitting dead ends, but she refused to let it dampen her resolve. There had to be something they were missing.

While the DNA was gathering matches, Lilly began to research the Big John bib Overalls bankruptcy.

"Okay, Liv, here it is. Big John struggled in the late '70s and early '80s, filing for bankruptcy protection multiple times. They eventually shut down."

Olivia let out a small gasp. "So, in 1982, the company was in rough straits. That might explain why we found the bib overalls with the male's remains. It seems like Big John was going through a bad period."

Lilly picked up her phone, ready to make a call. "I think it's worth reaching out to Big John's headquarters. We need to find out more about the status of the company during that time, the challenges they were facing, and if any records exist regarding the distribution of their products."

Olivia nodded in agreement.

Lilly picked up the phone, put it on speaker, and dialed the number. After a few rings, a receptionist answered the call in a cheerful tone.

"Big John Brands, how can I assist you?" the receptionist asked.

Lilly took a deep breath and introduced herself. "I was hoping to speak with someone who may have information about the company's status in 1982 & 1983."

The receptionist listened attentively and replied, "Let me transfer you to our archives department. They might have the information you're looking for. Please hold."

As Lilly waited, she exchanged a hopeful glance with Olivia. After a few minutes, a voice finally came through.

"Hello, this is the archives department. How can I help you?" a male voice greeted her.

Lilly introduced herself again and explained the purpose of her call. "We're particularly interested in any records or information about the company's situation in 1982 or 1983 that might shed some light on how this person came to own the pair of overalls."

The archivist took a moment to gather their thoughts before responding. "Well, in 1982, Big John was facing financial difficulties. The company had filed for bankruptcy protection and subsequently shut down. It was a challenging time for us."

Lilly quickly jotted notes. "Do you have any records of the distribution of your products during that period? Specifically, were the bib overalls widely available, or were they limited in their reach?"

The archivist sighed. "Unfortunately, we don't have specific distribution records from that time. However, I can tell you that Big John products were widely sold across the United States. They were particularly popular in blue-collar communities and areas with a strong workwear culture."

Lilly's curiosity got the best of her. "Were there any notable changes or events that occurred within the company during that period? Anything that might have impacted the availability or perception of the bib overalls?"

The archivist filled her in. "After the bankruptcy filings, Big John underwent a period of reevaluation. The company recognized the need to adapt to changing market trends and expand its product line. They wanted to appeal to a broader audience beyond the traditional workwear sector. Depending on when he came into possession of them, they might have been for sale or not. Production did stop for a considerable time period."

Olivia's eyes widened as she absorbed the information. "So, they were trying to diversify their offerings and reach a wider market. That's interesting. It could explain how the bib overalls made their way into the hands of our person."

The archivist responded, grasping her line of thinking. "That's a possibility. Big John made efforts to modernize its image and tap into emerging fashion trends. They aimed to appeal to a younger demographic, even collaborating with designers and featuring their products on runways."

Lilly had no idea the overalls were such a fashionable item. "Wow, that's fascinating! The bib overalls went from farm to fashionable. It's amazing how things change."

The archivist expressed his appreciation for their interest and offered further assistance if needed. Lilly thanked him and ended the call. Turning to Olivia, she couldn't help but feel hopeful.

"Olivia, this information opens up new possibilities for our investigation. The bib overalls represent not just workwear but also a symbol of changing fashion and cultural shifts. Oh my goodness, our Doe could be any man and every man!!!"

While here, there, and everywhere, it seemed, Olivia and Lilly were determined to make the most of their last night in Las Vegas before flying out in the morning. They had decided to treat themselves to a memorable evening, experiencing the best the city had to offer.

As they discussed their plans, Olivia suggested, "How about catching a captivating magic show? It would be a perfect way to end our time here."

Lilly's eyes lit up, "That sounds fantastic! I've always been intrigued by magic shows. Let's go for it!"

They quickly checked for available shows and secured tickets to a top-rated performance on the Strip. With their plans set, they headed to the theater.

The show lived up to its reputation, leaving them in awe with every illusion and sleight of hand. They couldn't help but cheer and applaud along with the rest of the audience as the magician wowed them with mind-boggling acts.

After the show, their hunger pangs kicked in, and they decided on a good meal to top off the night. Olivia suggested a trendy restaurant known for its good food and great atmosphere.

As they settled into the cozy ambiance of the restaurant, they browsed through the menu. "I've heard their seafood dishes are amazing," Olivia said, her eyes scanning the choices.

Lilly agreed, "You know what happens when I 'see food' and perhaps I'll indulge in a decadent dessert to celebrate our last supper."

The food turned out to be as delicious as they had hoped, and they relished every bite.

As the night came to a close, Olivia and Lilly strolled back to their hotel. They got organized, got settled, and tried to drift off to a peaceful sleep.

CHAPTER EIGHT

The morning sun cast a golden glow over Desert Oasis as Olivia and Lilly emerged from the hotel, excited but weary. As Olivia's mom used to say, 'It's nice to get away, but always good to come home.' They had a flight to catch, and their minds were already shifting gears, transitioning from the bustling city and the investigation to what awaited them back home.

As they drove to the rental car return, their conversation was filled with reflections on their time in Nevada. They chuckled at the memory of strange encounters with eccentric characters they had met along the way.

Olivia looked over and grinned at Lilly. "You know, Las Vegas is a show unto itself. The characters we came across were straight out of la la land!"

Lilly chuckled. "Definitely the perfect place for people-watching!"

They both cracked up, energizing their tired bodies. The rental car return was swift, and they made their way to the airport, navigating the crowds with ease.

As they settled into their seats on the plane, exhaustion began to creep back in. They exchanged a knowing glance, silently acknowledging their need for a well-deserved nap. With their heads against the headrests, they succumbed to the gentle hum of the aircraft, drifting into a peaceful slumber.

The flight itself was uneventful, the sky outside the window a vast expanse of blue. They woke briefly when the flight attendants passed by with drink carts.

Olivia nudged Lilly, "Remember when they used to serve real meals on planes? Now it's just tiny bags of peanuts or pretzels."

Lilly nodded, a wistful smile on her face. "Oh, those were the days. I remember sitting down to a proper meal with real silverware and a choice of entrees. It felt like a luxury, even in the air. Now, you're lucky if you can bring your suitcase."

They spent the rest of the long flight in peaceful silence, the rhythmic hum of the engines lulling them back to sleep.

The plane touched down, and Olivia and Lilly stirred awake, the weariness of their journey clinging to their bones. While jet setting across the United States was fun, it many times took almost all day, and then some. Jet lag was definitely making an appearance.

As they walked through the airport terminal, their eyes met, and they exchanged a knowing smile. They retrieved their luggage, hailed a taxi, and soon found themselves on their different doorsteps, the comforting familiarity of home welcoming them back. They stepped into their respective homes, ready to rest and recharge before the next chapter of their investigation began.

The next morning, Olivia had awoken early, checking once again to see if the DNA results were in. It was always hard being patient while waiting on the DNA, knowing that it held the key to the unknown male's identity. They both personally had experienced the power of genetic genealogy, a cutting-edge technique that utilized DNA to trace familial connections and build family trees. It had never let them down and they were always impatient to get started.

Olivia had just arrived at the office and was booting up when Victoria dropped by. She let Olivia know she had completed the tree for Jennifer and had sent the link for Olivia's review. Lilly followed not soon after and the ladies filled Victoria in on the new case, and she said she was available if they needed an extra set of hands.

Victoria left and Olivia anxiously refreshed the web pages for the databases to see if the matches had materialized. They hadn't.

The minutes ticked by as Olivia and Lilly sat staring at each other in the office. The air was thick with anticipation and the aroma of freshly brewed coffee. The air conditioner was on and the laptops were fully charged.

Olivia fidgeted with her chair. "You know, it's truly re-markable how far we've come with genetic genealogy. I still remember the day we first crossed paths, when you were looking to find Rosie's father."

Lilly nodded. "I know, it feels like a lifetime ago, huh? I had exhausted every avenue, hitting brick walls at every turn. I was losing hope."

"But then, fate intervened," Olivia interjected. "We stumbled into that genealogy group, and it was like the universe had conspired to guide us toward each other."

Lilly's face lit up as memories flooded back. "Yes, that was the turning point. I remember the sheer disbelief when you were able to find him in just two hours. It was a breakthrough that changed everything. Both for me as a mother, and for me as a career."

Olivia chuckled. "Your reaction was priceless, Lilly. You couldn't believe that we had found the missing piece of the puzzle just like that and that Rosie finally had the chance to know her biological father."

Lilly's eyes got moist. "It had been weighing me down for so long. And it ignited a passion within me to become a Forensic Genetic Genealogist and enroll in your class!"

Olivia's gaze fixed on Lilly. "And who could have imagined, after all that, our DNA research would reveal we're also distant cousins—it's a crazy twist of fate!"

Lilly broke into a huge grin. "As you say, 'You can't make this stuff up!'"

Olivia took a deep breath and let it out. "You know, there's something profound about those moments when you just know. I try to explain it to people. When you feel deep in your bones that you're on the right path. Like when we found Rosie's dad, or when we discovered our own familial connection. And, as you well know, when the DNA revealed the truth me."

Lilly understood. "It's that intuitive sense of certainty that fuels our investigations. It's like the universe whispers in our ears, guiding us toward the answers we seek. Now, if the universe can just hurry up with those matches too!"

Olivia laughed and checked the inbox, exclaiming, "What do you know? You did it, they're here!"

As they carefully studied the match lists, as always, they were struck by the wealth of information there. Charts and graphs depicted people who were biological genetic matches, and in this instance, offering clues to the unknown Doe's ancestry. The report also categorized these matches, using references based on centimorgans or cMs, outlining the amount of DNA shared between the two. It was the information in these matches, that guided Olivia and Lilly in their work to identify the Doe.

Olivia wanted to focus her attention on the matches that might have a connection to Desert Oasis or the route of the Union Pacific Railway. But first, they had to follow the golden rule of identifying the highest centimorgan matches and building their family trees.

As usual, some matches were in one database while others were in another. Of the big industry players, only two allowed law enforcement matching. Gathering the match information from the two, Olivia and Lilly took turns writing them on the whiteboard, highest to lowest, for easy visual reference as they built those matches' trees.

"The first is Daniel Murphy," Lilly said as she wrote, "He's a suggested first to second match to our Doe at 799 cMs."

"Wow, that's such a good match, and, I've got a Chris Murphy," Olivia said excitedly. "He's a close cousin match to our Doe with 443 cMs, also a suggested first to second cousin. Our Doe could be a Murphy! But, we know about making assumptions, right?"

"Oh, we certainly do!" Lilly emphasized.

"I've got a 394 next, what do you have?" Olivia said.

"392 so you're still up," Lilly responded.

Olivia added Karen Riley to the list with 394 cMs as a potential first to second cousin.

Lilly nodded, "That's a good one," she said, "And Dorothy Burton a reported first to second cousin match with 392 cMs. That's a significant connection too," she added it to the board. And I've got Pat Allen, a suggested second to third cousin with 263."

Olivia was up next. "M. Ryan, a suggested second to third cousin match with 110 CM. That's still a significant amount of shared DNA," she noted, "But, no amount is too small for me," she said with a smile.

Lilly's gaze fell upon the next and final names on the list. "Donna Stevens, possibly a fourth to sixth cousin at 44 cMs, and E. Smith, a possible fourth to sixth cousin match with 44 CM," she noted, adding them to the board. "Though more distant, they could still provide clues about the John Doe's family tree, help us confirm identity and potentially lead us to uncover additional relatives."

With the matches organized by "cousinness" as Olivia liked to call it, they then followed Olivia's process and started building trees for the highest matches first. After a few hours, they needed to get up and walk and went out into the neighborhood surrounding the office. Sitting too long at the computer takes its toll and Olivia made a joke of it saying, "You know I'm dedicated to my job. I've got the extra 50 pounds to prove it." Between the DNA drama, the recent death of her mother, and the endless computer work, this was the one battle where Olivia had decided to waive the white flag. At least for now.

As they strolled through the quaint downtown area near their office, Lilly broke the silence. "You know, based on what we've seen in the trees we've been building, I'd say our John Doe was probably born in the 1930s."

Olivia nodded, "That fits with the estimated age at death, somewhere between 35 to 50 years old. Based on the relative matches I'm working it seems his family is deeply rooted in Chicago."

Lilly looked thoughtful. Yeah, I'm kinda getting the same thing. If I remember my history correctly, the 1930s were a pivotal time in Chicago's history. It was the era of the Great

Depression, but also the time of the World's Fair: Century of Progress, which took place in 1933 and 1934."

Olivia glanced at Lilly, intrigued, "You, the history buff. Wasn't the fair supposed to be a symbol of hope and innovation amidst the struggles of the times?"

Lilly confirmed it adding, "And if John Doe was born during that time, imagine the kind of life he would have had. Growing up, he would have seen Chicago transform post-Depression and then during the World War II years."

"Hmmmm," Olivia chimed in. "And it's plausible that John Doe's family, like many other families at that time, stayed rooted in the area, despite the economic hardships."

Lilly thought about the Windy City. "Fast-forward to today and Chicago is this bustling city full of opportunities. It's amazing to think about how much it has changed and how these families, and others like it, played a role in that."

"Chicago wasn't the only city going through changes in the 1930s," Olivia said, breaking the silence. "Think about Las Vegas, where we just were."

Lilly remembered. "That's true! Las Vegas was just a speck in the desert back then, wasn't it?"

Olivia nodded, "Las Vegas was pretty much a small railroad town until the construction of Hoover Dam in the early 30s. That brought thousands of workers to the area. I remember this from when I lived in Arizona."

Lilly added, "And then there was the legalization of gambling in 1931. It fundamentally transformed Las Vegas from a sleepy town into an emerging entertainment hub."

"Right," Olivia agreed, "So while our Doe's family was living through the Great Depression in Chicago, the West was on the brink of a major transformation. It's fascinating to think how different his life could have been had his family moved to Las Vegas instead."

The comparison to Las Vegas put their investigation into perspective. Every city, like every family, had its own unique history. Understanding these broader historical contexts helped Olivia and Lilly appreciate the complex tapestry of John Doe's life and times. Exactly like the pieces to a puzzle, they couldn't wait to see the final picture.

Back in the office, Olivia saw a missed call from Agent Beck from the Postal Inspector's office. She called her right back.

"Agent Beck," she asked, excitedly. "Do you have any up-dates for us?"

Agent Beck did. "I've been going through our records, and I managed to find a potential match for the partial surname on the monogram," she revealed. "There was a postal employee named Harold Radcliffe who worked in the Las Vegas area during that time."

Olivia's eyes got huge and she poked Lilly. "Harold Rad-cliffe? That's a huge lead," she replied. "Can you pro-vide any additional information on this person? Is he still alive?"

Agent Beck paused for a moment. "I'm afraid I don't have anything else. It's weird, not a lot of records were kept but I'm finding bits and pieces from old documents scanned and uploaded to the server. All I have is the name, and it's attached to the Desert Oasis office," she told her.

"Well, Ancestry.com is a big repository of data and I can see what we can do to find the information. I'll let Desert Oasis PD know. We got the DNA in and we are starting to work on it. I'll definitely let you know if I'm able to find any Radcliffe's."

Agent Beck sounded relieved. "That's great to hear. I believe this could be a significant breakthrough," she acknowledged. "Please keep me updated."

"Absolutely," Olivia assured her. "Thank you so much for your help. We'll be in touch soon."

After hanging up, Olivia turned to Lilly, who had been listening to the call. "Well, I want to say I'm excited about this breakthrough from Agent Beck, but at the same time, there seems to be nary a speck of Scotland in my DNA matches. And nothing right now in Vegas."

Lilly had a forlorn look on her face. "The best-laid, plans of genetic genealogists...", she drifted off.

"Time will tell," Olivia said, "And speaking of which, I'm ready to call it a day."

"Me too, I'm right behind you," Lilly said as she closed her laptop, got her purse, and headed out.

CHAPTER NINE

O livia entered the office the next morning, her eyes tired from a restless night. She found Lilly sitting at the desk, surrounded by papers and a laptop, her face also etched with exhaustion. Lilly looked up, a mixture of relief and disappointment evident in her eyes.

"Lilly, you look like you've been up all night," Olivia remarked, concern lacing her voice. "What's going on?"

Lilly let out a sigh and gestured to the papers spread out before her. "I couldn't sleep. I had to dig deeper into the Harold Radcliffe lead. It seemed so good, but it wasn't making sense. Unfortunately, it seems we've hit a dead end."

Olivia approached the desk. "What do you mean? Did you find the right Harold Radcliffe?"

Lilly shook her head, her voice tinged with frustration. "Not quite. I did locate a Harold Radcliffe who moved to Las Vegas in 1992, but his family history doesn't align with what we know about the Doe. The Harold I found has a Scottish and Eurasian background, but our DNA results aren't pointing in that direction."

Olivia leaned against the desk, reviewing Lilly's tree. "So, it's a different Harold Radcliffe then?"

Lilly nodded, disappointment evident in her expression. "Well, this might be THE Harold Radcliffe that worked for the post office but it can't be our John Doe. This Harold's mother is Ethiopian, married to a Scot. Given his family heritage, the ethnicity doesn't fit. And neither does the timing. The Doe's disappearance dates back to 1983, long before this Harold's move to Las Vegas."

Olivia sighed, feeling the weight of the setback. "I was hoping we had finally found a solid lead. It seemed too good to be true."

Lilly's eyes met Olivia's. "But this doesn't mean we're back to square one. It just means we need to keep digging, exploring different avenues, and considering alternative possibilities."

Olivia nodded. "We can't let this setback discourage us. It's all part of the process. There's still more to uncover, more connections to explore. We owe it to the Doe to never give up."

Olivia took a deep breath, her fingers gently tapping on the desk as she glanced at Lilly, who was still absorbed in her research. She knew it was time to make the call to Chief Thompson at the Desert Oasis PD. She wished she had better news.

Olivia reached for her phone, dialing the number. After a few rings, the chief's voice came through the line.

"Chief Thompson speaking."

"Chief, it's Olivia Mason. I wanted to update you on our findings regarding the John Doe case," Olivia said.

The chief seemed excited. "Oh, great to hear from you, go ahead. What have you found?"

Olivia took a breath and exhaled loudly. "Well, we've made progress on several fronts. We researched the partial monogram on the postal shirt, which led us to reach out to the Postal Inspector's office. Agent Beck there helped us identify a potential lead, Harold Radcliffe."

Olivia continued, giving him the details on the timing, and moved on to the fact that they did get the genome back and were doing preliminary work on the most favorable matches. "However, our recent DNA results are not pointing in the direction of Harold's genetic composition. So, it's a dead end at this time, no pun intended. Agent Beck, though, did all she could and was not able to find any employee with the '...IFFE' in their name. I don't know where that places us, except that maybe it's a fake name used for a sample or something like that. I haven't really fleshed all of that out yet. I just wanted to touch base and let you know where we are."

There was a brief pause on the other end of the line, and Olivia could almost hear the chief processing the information. Finally, he spoke. "I appreciate your thoroughness. We do need to explore every avenue. Even if Harold isn't our guy, there may be other leads to follow. Let's continue to share our findings and keep going. We can't afford to lose momentum."

Olivia nodded, "I hear you, Chief. We'll keep working and update you with any new developments."

As Olivia ended the call, she glanced at Lilly, their eyes meeting in a shared understanding. They may not have found the breakthrough they had hoped for, but the game was far from over.

Lilly leaned back in her chair, spinning around to face Olivia. "Okay, on a good note, I've been digging into Daniel Murphy's family history, and it's fascinating. His roots in Chicago run deep, and his family has quite the story."

Olivia looked at her with curiosity. "What did you find?"

Lilly adjusted her glasses and began. "Well, it seems that Daniel's mother, Jeannie O'Connor, comes from a prominent Irish-American family with strong ties to the city. They were well-known in the construction industry, and her father, Edward O'Connor, had quite the reputation. Oh, and Jeannie is the grandmother of Chris Murphy, our 443."

Olivia was, eager to hear more. "Cool! What did Edward do?"

"He was a construction mogul, Lilly replied, her voice laced with admiration. "Edward built a thriving business from the ground up, specializing in residential and com-

mercial projects. Apparently, his craftsmanship and expertise are part of many iconic Chicago landmarks."

Olivia's eyes lit up, a realization dawning on her. "The
construction background and the connections to Chicago...the construction industry could be something to look
into."

Lilly agreed. "Mmmhmm. I thought it was interesting. I've
got more."

"Now, Karen Riley's family has a strong presence in the
Chicago area as well. Her roots can be traced back to a long
line of hardworking folks who played significant roles in
the city's industrial landscape."

Olivia was surprised. "Industrial? What kind of industries
are we talking about?"

Lilly nodded excitedly. "Karen's paternal side of the family
was involved in the steel industry. Her great-grandfather,
James Riley, owned a successful steel manufacturing company. It was known for producing high-quality steel products that were in demand across the region."

Olivia worked to connect the dots in her mind. "Gosh,
the steel industry too could be a crucial piece of our Doe's

story too. If he had ties to Karen's family, it's possible he was involved in the steel industry as well."

Lilly was reviewing her notes. "That's right. The family's legacy in the steel industry could shed light on our Doe's background, occupation, or even potential connections to other individuals in that field. I hate to say it but it seems we have a lot of big business here in a big city and we have the missing body parts. Could we be dancing around organized crime again?"

Olivia noted the details. "Gosh, I hope not. Let's research these family histories. We need to explore the steel and construction industry networks, and any significant events or partnerships.

"Umm, have you been able to place Dorothy Burton yet?" Olivia asked.

Lilly flipped through the pages of her research. "Yes, let me see. Dorothy's family hails from the Chicago area as well. They were quote 'prominent players' in the cultural and artistic scene."

Olivia seemed surprised. "Cultural and artistic? Wow, we seem to have hit the mother load of talent here in these relatives. That's so fascinating. What did they do in the arts?"

Lilly nodded, a smile playing on her lips. "I know, crazy, huh? Dorothy's maternal great-grandfather, Walter Stevens, was an accomplished painter and sculptor. He was renowned for his breathtaking landscapes and captivating sculptures that captured the essence of Chicago."

Olivia's eyes sparkled with curiosity. "Man, to be in that family! Did he have any notable achievements or recognition?"

Lilly nodded. "He sure did! Walter Steven's works were showcased in prestigious galleries and exhibitions throughout the city. He received numerous accolades and was 'highly regarded among the artistic community' end quote."

Olivia was connecting the dots in her mind. "The artistic background of Dorothy's family is another avenue of possibilities for our John Doe. Man, reminds me of Harborville. I wonder if our Doe was talented too?"

Lilly nodded. "Yes, remember what we learned there? The artistic community often fosters close-knit relationships and collaborations. Exploring Dorothy's family connections could lead us to people who knew our John Doe or were familiar with any artistic pursuits."

"Great work, Lilly," Olivia said. "We need to look into that but we also have some unfinished business with the Post Office."

During their prior research on the postal uniforms, they found a few former employees who worked at Yeager Uniform during the 70s and 80s. Some had retired and were spread across the country. They had compiled a list of potential contacts and reached out to them. One of the names was Margaret Sullivan. She had been a seamstress at Yeager, specializing in postal uniforms. Olivia had scheduled a Zoom call with her previously and it was just about that time.

Olivia glanced at her watch, feeling a mixture of anticipation and nerves. "Martha should be online any minute. I hope she's open to sharing her experiences with us."

Lily was thoughtful. "I have a feeling she'll be willing to talk. After all, she was a part of Yaeger Uniform during a significant time. She might hold the missing puzzle piece that could bring us closer to solving this case."

Just as Lily finished speaking, an elderly woman with silver hair and a warm smile came online. "Hi! I'm Martha," she said, waving her hand in greeting.

Olivia and Lily waved too, returning the smile. "It's a pleasure to meet you, Martha," Olivia said. "Thank you for taking the time to meet with us."

Martha adjusted her monitor nervously. "I must admit, I was surprised when you reached out to me. It's been years since I've thought about my time at Yeager Uniform."

Olivia began. "We're conducting an investigation regarding an unidentified deceased man found near Jackrabbit Mountain, in Desert Oasis, in Nevada back in 1983. The case has crossed paths with Yeager postal uniforms and the Yeager uniform jackets. We were hoping you could share any insights or memories you have related to those jackets."

Martha's expression went from shocked to thoughtful as she took a sip of her tea. "Wow, okay. Ah, the Yeager jackets. I remember them well. The postal service was one of our biggest clients, and we took great pride in crafting those uniforms."

Olivia perked up, eager to hear more. "Did you have any specific memories or encounters related to the jackets,

Martha? Anything that might help us identify the man found on Jackrabbit Mountain?"

Martha's eyes were distant as she thought back. "Nevada, huh? We're based in Kansas City. Well, I recall there was a period when we had a few traveling salespeople on our team. They would visit post offices across the country, promoting the quality and durability of our uniforms. I can't say for certain if they had any connection to the unidentified man, but it's worth looking into."

Lily piped up from her notetaking. "Thank you, Martha. This is important information. Do you happen to remember the names of any of those traveling salespeople? It could help us track down leads."

Martha tapped her chin, a look of concentration on her face. "There was a young man, Tom, who worked as a salesman for a while. I'm afraid I don't remember his last name though. I believe he traveled quite a lot, visiting different post offices in various states though he was based out of Kansas. He was quite charismatic, always had a way with people."

Olivia and Lily exchanged glances. "Tom could be a good lead," Olivia said. "We'll make sure to check his connection to the Yeager jackets and the unidentified man. Thank you, Martha. This has been really helpful."

Lilly wanted to make sure they didn't forget the partial name and asked, "Can you tell us how the monograms were created?"

Martha took a moment to gather her thoughts before responding. "Well, back in those days, we used a combination of machine and hand embroidery to create the monograms. Each employee's name was stitched onto their uniforms to personalize them."

Lilly let out an excited Oh and went on. "Were there any instances where sample names or initials were used on the uniforms that the salesmen took around?"

Martha nodded, a faint smile playing on her lips. "Ah, yes, the sample uniforms. We did have a few with generic names or initials stitched on them. They were used to demonstrate the quality of our work to potential clients."

Olivia cautiously broached the next question, "Martha, this will sound weird and maybe uncomfortable, but we found a set of postal uniforms with the John Doe in the desert. The postal inspector's office said they could not find any employees with that name combination. Well, they found one but he was not an employee until way later. Anyhow, on the shirts found at the scene, there was a partial monogram, missing most of the first letters, except for '...IFFE'. We've Googled all kinds of combinations and are coming up empty. Would that make any kind of sense to you?"

Both Olivia and Lilly were a bit freaked out when all of a sudden, Martha started laughing to the point she started crying. "Oh, my, goodness, ladies. I can't tell you what that does for me. I have not thought of Billy in forever." She paused to get her composure.

Olivia and Lilly looked at each other, not knowing what to expect next.

Martha went on. "Okay, my apologies, and now I have to say that this will sound weird but it was a 'big', pun intended inside joke. I forget when it was, but for several months we had been receiving uniform requests, custom, for really, really large sizes. Gosh, I hope I can explain this right. Billy was a huge fan of history and he would remark on how big the postal employees were getting and how they must be 'bulging' out all over." She started laughing again and had to take a breath.

Olivia and Lilly still didn't know what to do and looked from each other to the screen and back to each other.

Finally, Martha was able to continue. "I mean no disrespect here but I'm focusing on Billy's weird sense of humor and fascination with war. Apparently when 'Bulge' came to mind in Billy's head, so too did some sort of military General I think, what was his name........McAuliffe, I think it was, who was at the 'Battle of the Bulge'. It just went on and on and on. In order to get Billy to shut up about it, we promised him we would memorialize 'the big guy' and sew the sample names as McAuliffe. I'm afraid that's all there is to it. I can't tell you how many uniform samples were made 'in honor' of the General."

Olivia nodded and said, "Oh, I see." She took a big pause and continued. "Were there any requirements about security and the return of the postal uniforms once the employee had left?"

"Well, I know we had to go through a very significant background check in order to work on the federal programs and we had detailed inventory about what was made and where it went. Outside of our department, I have no idea." Martha added.

Lilly nodded appreciatively. "Thank you, Martha. We'll definitely look into those leads. This was really helpful. If we have any more questions, would it be alright if we reach out to you?"

Martha smiled, a sense of satisfaction evident in her eyes. "Yes, most definitely. I'm glad I could help. That's a long time going unrecognized, the poor man. Good luck. I hope you find the answers you're looking for."

As Martha bid them farewell and left the meeting, Olivia and Lily remained at the table, engrossed in their conversation. "We have a name to pursue now," Lilly said, her voice tinged with excitement. "Tom, the charismatic sales representative." We need to find out more about his travels, and his interactions with post offices, and if there's any connection to our John Doe."

"Yes," Olivia said, "It seems that since we don't have any employees that fit the monogram, though, it's looking more and more like a sample. Maybe Tom is our John Doe?"

CHAPTER TEN

A rriving in the office the next morning, the ladies were hoping to get lucky with Tom, in the DNA sense. They hoped that they might find a Tom, in the Kansas area, who was originally from Chicago and looked to be a lot Irish. Without a last name, or anything to go on, they would have to hope that the link might reveal itself in the DNA matches or their family.

When working on police cases, unfortunately, only two commercial DNA databases provided access for law enforcement matching. Lilly took one and Olivia the other, working to sort the matches into paternal and maternal sides, which enabled them to be more efficient and accurate in identifying the most recent common ancestors.

From the tree information, they found that Daniel Murphy, Chris Murphy, M. Ryan, and Evan Smith all descended from the same biological family with their most common recent ancestors John O'Connor and Bridget Boyle. Without any connections, and on the opposite side of the tree, they had Dorothy Burton, Patricia Allen, and Donna Stevens. Now they had to build out their family trees and follow the roadmap, looking for the connection.

Olivia took the Murphy-linked matches and Lilly took the Burton clan. They built out the trees and then located the possibilities based on the shared centimorgans. They had a few to choose from.

Making sure to get it straight, Olivia began to detail her tree for Lilly, who was drawing it out on the whiteboard in the office. Olivia stood up, papers in hand, and began to recount, "Okay, here we go Edward O'Connor, born in 1883, should be the purported father of the John Doe. Jeannie O'Connor, who is Edward's daughter, is Daniel Murphy's mom. Bridget Boyle is Edward's wife and Jeannie's mother. In addition to Daniel, Jeannie had another son, Jack Murphy, who is the father of Chris Murphy."

Olivia looked up as Lilly was making squares, drawing lines, and nodding, "Yep. Got more?"

"I do," Olivia continued. "Okay, so Edward O'Connor, his father was Patrick O'Connor, circa 1850, and Patrick's dad was John O'Connor." She took a breath. "John O'Connor Senior had a son, John O'Connor Junior. Junior had two daughters, Mabel and Lillian. Lillian is the mother of M. Ryan. Mabel married a Smith and had a son James Smith, who had a son Richard Smith, who had a son, Evan Smith. Oops, I forgot...."

"Wait a sec, I'm getting lost in the offspring." Lilly said.

"Are you ready?" Asked Olivia, and when given the go-ahead, continued. "Okay, back to Edward. His wife is Bridget Boyle, mom of Jeannie, right? Well, Bridget had a brother, Joseph Riley, who had a son, Lawrence Riley, and Lawrence had Karen. I think that is all of our good matches on that side."

Lilly finished up, walked over and handed the marker to Olivia and picked up her notes. "Alrighty, then. Dorothy Burton, her mother is Eileen Stevens, circa 1931. Eileen was the namesake of her mother, Eileen Senior, circa 1906. Eileen Senior was the daughter of Walter Stevens, circa 1870. Are you with me?"

"One sec," Olivia added, erasing and filling in. "Okay, I'm good."

"So, Walter Stevens, he had another daughter, Lydia, circa 1908. I believe Lydia is the mother of our Doe. We also have William, circa 1872, who is the brother of Walter Stevens. William had his namesake, William Junior, circa 1896, who had a son Cyril, who had a daughter, our match Donna." She waited for a beat and then, "Last but not least, we have Patricia Allen. Her mother is Jenny Owens, daughter of William Owens, who is the brother of Mary Owens, Walter Steven's wife and Lydia Stevens' mother. Gosh, it's so much easier to see it visually."

"You got that right!" Olivia added.

They then used their roadmap, comparing the centimorgans to make sure it all fit perfectly, just like puzzle pieces to reveal the right picture. They each checked, rechecked, and viewed genealogical records and trees.

Olivia went first. "I have Edward O'Connor as father and Lydia Stevens as mother. This is based on the cM values on the O'Connor side that appear to support half relationships between our Doe and Jeannie O'Connor."

Lilly nodded, confirming, "Yep."

Olivia continued, "Based on that, we have Edward married to Ann Riley first and then a second marriage to Lydia, producing seven offspring. A nod to what my mother liked to call 'being a good Catholic.'"

"I'm good, keep going," Lilly said.

"So, from that union, we have the seven offspring, four of which are boys. Edward, circa 1935, Robert, circa 1937, Patrick, circa 1938, and Richard, circa 1939. Now we just have to research those boys and see if we can easily tell who's still with us." Olivia added.

Lilly sarcastically added, "Don't I wish it was that easy!"

Olivia suddenly remembered, "Hey wait, I guess it's not Tom here, our salesman, right? Did I miss a kid somewhere?"

Appearing downtrodden, Lilly replied, "No, you did not. And that throws our Doe as a traveling salesperson right out the window."

"One down, a few thousand to go!" Exclaimed Olivia as she sat down. "I don't know about you but I'm about over it today. Whaddya say we start back fresh tomorrow."

Lilly easily agreed.

While it was exciting that they were really close, the rise and fall, the near and far, and the almost but and no cigar took its toll, sooner than one would think. Genetic genealogy involved a lot of computer time, reading, theorizing, mouse clicking and you never knew when you were going to hit the wall. Until you did. And that's when they crashed.

Lilly was out the door first, followed quickly by Olivia saying goodbye to the relatives and hello to blissful sleep.

In the kitchen at the office the next morning, Olivia and Lilly were discussing where they were with the case. "It's time to update Chief Thompson again on our progress," Olivia said. "I forgot to tell him about our conversation with Martha, the former Yeager employee, and our ruling out of the salesman theory based on location, DNA matches, and ethnicity. And, of course, we have some exciting news about our potential identification of John Doe as one of the O'Connor siblings."

Lilly nodded. "I'm excited. Can we also ask for approval to reach out to the O'Connor family for further assistance to help narrow down the brothers?"

Getting the chief on the phone, Olivia took a deep breath and began. "Chief Thompson, we have some significant updates on the case. We were able to speak to a former Yeager employee who shed some light on the monograms." She filled him in on the name not belonging to a real person and referenced Martha's remembrance of Tom the traveling salesman. "It looked good at first, however, we have ruled out the possibility of a salesman connection through the DNA matches."

Lilly went next. "Chief, all is not lost though. We've been doing extensive genealogical research, and we believe we have narrowed down John Doe as one of the O'Connor siblings from Chicago. However, we still need to solidify the identification and determine which brother it might be. Are you okay with us reaching out to the closer relatives and trying to get more information on the family? Of course, we would not make any notification."

Chief Thompson let out a huge sigh and said, "Wow, great job, ladies. I know how hard you've been working on this case. If you feel reaching out to the highest DNA matches in the O'Connor family will provide what we need, I fully support your plan. Yes, death notifications are not fun, as you are probably well aware and we like to approach any close relationship with kid gloves."

Olivia smiled gratefully. "Thank you, Chief. We'll proceed with contacting the O'Connor family for background and keep you posted. While we still have no idea what our Doe was doing, we do believe we will have his name shortly."

The Chief added, "Keep up the good work. Remember, my door is always open."

"Will do, sir. Talk to you soon." Olivia added and hung up the phone.

Next on the schedule was speaking to Agent Beck at the Postal Inspector's office. Now that they had four possible names, they felt it might make Beck's job easier.

Olivia anxiously dialed the number, her fingers tapping against the table as the phone rang. After a few moments, Agent Beck's voice crackled through the line.

"Agent Beck speaking. How can I assist you?" Beck's voice held the no-nonsense tone of a seasoned investigator.

"Agent Beck, this is Olivia Mason again. We've made a significant discovery regarding the unidentified man. We have four possible names associated with him, pending final DNA confirmation; they are Edward O'Connor, circa 1935, Robert O'Connor, circa 1937, Patrick O'Connor, circa 1938, and Richard O'Connor, circa 1939. All appear to have originated in the Chicago or Midwest area," Olivia relayed, her voice hopeful.

"Wow, great news! That genetic genealogy is doing great things." There was a momentary pause on the other end, and Olivia could almost feel the wheels turning in Beck's mind. Finally, Beck responded, her voice tinged with curiosity, "Hmm, all O'Connor's, you say? Let me check my database and see if there's any information on them. Hold on a sec."

Olivia, as usual, had a hard time being patient as she waited for Beck to return to the phone.

A few minutes later, Beck's voice came back, a note of surprise apparent. "Olivia, you won't believe this. I've found something! While we don't have a Richard O'Connor as a missing postal employee, we do have a record of unclaimed mail, via general delivery from 1983, in Desert Oasis addressed to a Richard O'Connor. It seems he had mail waiting for him but never claimed it."

Olivia could not believe it. "Unclaimed mail? That's interesting. What do you think the odds are that it's our Richard O'Connor? So it means a Richard O'Connor had a presence in Desert Oasis in 1983? What does general delivery mean in this case?" Olivia inquired.

Beck's voice on the other end carried a hint of amusement. "Sure. General delivery is a service provided by the postal service where individuals can have mail sent to a specific post office rather than a specific address. The recipient can then pick up the mail by presenting proper identification at the designated post office."

Olivia nodded, mentally processing the information. "So, if Richard O'Connor had mail waiting for him in Desert Oasis, it means he had intentionally sent something there or was expecting something to be sent to that location."

Beck chimed in, elaborating on the possibilities. "You've got it. It could indicate that Richard O'Connor had a connection to Desert Oasis, whether it be for personal or business reasons. Unclaimed mail of that nature often suggests a change of plans or unforeseen circumstances on the recipient's end."

Olivia contemplated the meaning. "Hmmm, it certainly raises more questions. Why didn't Richard O'Connor claim the mail? Was there something that prevented him from doing so? Or did he simply abandon the idea altogether?"

Beck responded thoughtfully. "That's what we're here to find out, right? We'll check into the unclaimed mail, and look for any additional records or clues that might shed light on what happened."

Olivia expressed her gratitude for Beck's continued efforts. "Thank you, Agent Beck. We really appreciate your help here. Please let us know if you find anything else."

Beck assured Olivia. "You have my word, Olivia. We're in this together. We'll figure it out, no matter how long it takes."

As Olivia hung up the phone, she turned to Lilly, and quickly filled her in.

Lilly smiled and did a little dance move. "We're getting closer. Let's dig into every lead and piece together the story of Richard O'Connor and Desert Oasis. I think he's our guy. I feel it. We are so close!"

CHAPTER ELEVEN

A rmed with the news about the General Delivery, Olivia and Lilly began to contemplate the connection between their Chicago Richard O'Connor and Desert Oasis.

"Okay, so we've narrowed it down by DNA that it has to be one of the O'Connor brothers, one of whom is a Richard O'Connor, born at the right time to be our dead guy. Now we have Agent Beck telling us that 'a' Richard O'Connor had unclaimed mail in Desert Oasis, exactly where our John Doe died, and it was delivered there in 1983." Lilly recounted. "Too bad we are not in Las Vegas right now because I think those are very great odds."

"I definitely agree and my gut says that it's him," Olivia replied. "So let's say it's him. It's interesting that Richard O'Connor and his relatives seem to have roots in Chicago, but we find him here in Nevada." Olivia mused. "What would have brought him all the way to Desert Oasis? What could have prompted him to embark on this journey?"

Lilly's eyes scanned the information they had gathered. "It's a question for sure. Maybe he was seeking new opportunities, a fresh start away from the familiarity of Chicago. Desert Oasis and Las Vegas have always held an allure for those searching for a different life, a chance to change their circumstances."

Olivia was thoughtful. "Yes, Las Vegas has often been associated with dreams, hopes, and aspirations. It's a city of reinvention, where one can try their luck in various industries, from entertainment to hospitality. But what led Richard to choose this particular path?"

Lilly gave it a go. "Maybe he was drawn to the excitement and energy of the West. The idea of something different, the allure of the unknown. It's hard to say, but there must have been a reason that called him to leave his familiar surroundings."

Olivia's gaze wandered, lost in her thoughts. "What if there were personal circumstances that drove him away? A longing for change, a desire to break free from the constraints of his previous life. Or maybe he was seeking something specific, something that only Desert Oasis could offer?"

Lilly nodded. "Whatever the reason, it's clear that Desert Oasis held significance for Richard O'Connor. The unclaimed mail, his journey to this city—it's all part of a bigger story waiting to be told."

Olivia sighed, "Well, we are talking about 1983 or 1982 even. What was going on back then in Chicago, Desert Oasis, and the United States?"

Lilly began to click the keyboard, and her mouse was flying as she researched online. Olivia joined her, scooting her chair over, eager to learn.

"Chicago, the early 1980s... a time of economic turmoil and uncertainty," Lilly murmured, her voice filled with a mix of curiosity and concern. "The recession hit hard, with high unemployment rates, layoffs, and struggling industries."

Olivia nodded, her eyes scanning the web pages before them. "Oh, geez. It must have been tough for many people in Chicago during that time. Limited job opportunities, financial hardships—it's no wonder some sought refuge or new beginnings elsewhere."

Lilly's read aloud, "Industries such as manufacturing, steel, and automotive faced significant declines, leading to widespread job losses. Many individuals found themselves struggling to make ends meet, searching for alternative ways to secure their livelihoods."

"And what about out west? What drew people like Richard O'Connor to places like Desert Oasis? Would it have been a better alternative?" Olivia asked.

Lilly's continued. "I think so, it says here that while the recession affected many parts of the country, some western states, like Nevada, experienced a different trajectory. The growth of tourism, entertainment, and the construction industry in Las Vegas and Desert Oasis created new job opportunities."

Olivia's voice rose with excitement. "So, Richard might have seen the glimmering lights of Vegas and the call of the West as a beacon of hope amidst the economic hardships in Chicago. A chance for a fresh start, a potential for finding work and stability."

Lilly nodded, her mind racing with possibilities. "Right! The allure of a booming city, the promise of employment, and the belief that the West held better prospects—it could have been a compelling reason for Richard to go there."

"Wait a minute," Olivia questioned Lilly, "Did you say that manufacturing and steel were down and they had job losses? Wasn't some of our supposed Richard's family involved in those industries?"

Lilly checked her notes. "Good catch, Liv. Yes, Edward O'Connor, the suspected father of Richard O'Connor was in the construction industry. He had passed by then but what if the sons, or one of them, was running the business? Maybe they fell on hard times?"

"Oooh, that's a great lead to follow. I think we need to explore the O'Connor boys and try to narrow our possibilities down first before we do any more supposing. We need to know which one we are dealing with. Let's hope that there's not a missing son in the mix like in my family!"

They huddled together to find contact information for the closest relatives and decided on a plan of attack.

Later, with that plan in place, Olivia taught her genetic genealogy class to the police, while Lilly was hot on the case, writing to emails listed in the DNA relatives' profiles, messaging on Facebook, and looking for phone numbers in their investigative databases. They focused on Dorothy Burton, Daniel Murphy, and Christopher Murphy.

After lunch, Olivia and Lilly were talking in the office kitchen when the phone rang. It was Agent Beck from the US Postal Service. Olivia raised a questioning eyebrow to Lilly and answered it.

"Olivia, I have some significant findings to share with you," Agent Beck replied, her tone filled with a mix of excitement and intrigue. "I managed to trace a list of cities that Richard O'Connor visited in the six months leading up to his stop in Desert Oasis. Well, I'm not sure he visited, but he had forwarded mail via General Delivery service."

Olivia's heart skipped a beat. This was the breakthrough they had been waiting for. "Oh wow! Sorry, please, go on."

Agent Beck continued. "Based on the records I obtained, it looks like our postal customer Richard did originate in Chicago. Agent Beck paused briefly before continuing. "I have a list of towns that Richard stayed in, albeit briefly, as he requested general delivery mail there. It appears he spent time in Des Moines, Iowa, Sydney, Nebraska, and Salt Lake City. The first stop, Des Moines, was forwarded from the 60611 zip code. That's in the heart of the city."

Olivia's voice was filled with excitement. "Thank you, Agent Beck. Oh my goodness, this is wonderful. We now have a glimpse into Richard's path as he went. Would you please send me the list in email?"

Agent Beck agreed, took down Olivia's email and they hung up.

Olivia and Lilly were so excited. This really pointed towards the fact that the Post Office identified 'Richard O'Connor' could be the DNA Richard O'Connor from Chicago they had found. They went back into Olivia's office to see if they could find Census information that matched.

"Oh, Liv, I forgot to tell you," Lilly said. "I heard back from Chris Murphy, Jeannie O'Connor's son, and we are

Zooming tomorrow. The meeting should be in your cal-
endar."

"So incredible, it's really all coming together, isn't it?"
Olivia responded.

Olivia and Lilly dove back into their investigation with
renewed focus, determined to narrow down the potential John Doe from the four brothers: Edward, Robert,
Patrick, and Richard. They spent hours combing through
records, cross-referencing information, and checking social media platforms to find any clues that could help them
identify the missing man.

Lilly started with Robert, looking into public records and
social media profiles to see if there were any signs of his
existence after the discovery of John Doe in 1983. As she
researched Robert O'Connor, born in 1937, her excitement grew. "Olivia, I think I've found something!" she
exclaimed as she scrolled through the search results on her
computer screen.

Olivia leaned over, eager to see what Lilly had uncovered.
"What is it?"

Lilly pointed to the screen, "I found records showing that
Robert got married and moved to Wisconsin after 1985.

It seems like he started a new chapter in his life there. Of course, we know not to trust the genealogy but it certainly looks promising."

"That's a great find!" Olivia replied, "It means he was alive and well after the time of John Doe's death."

Lilly nodded, "Exactly. And that's not all. I found information suggesting that he might be buried in Mt. Carmel cemetery right here in Chicago. There's even a picture of his gravestone on FindAGrave."

Olivia's eyes widened with surprise and relief. "That's a crucial piece of evidence! If we can confirm that Robert is indeed buried in Mt. Carmel cemetery, it would eliminate him as a potential match for the John Doe in Desert Oasis."

As they continued their investigation, they verified the information, cross-referencing it with official records and contacting the cemetery for confirmation. The more they dug, the more certain they became that Robert O'Connor, born in 1937, was indeed alive after the Doe went missing, had continued his life, passed on, and was buried in Mt. Carmel cemetery.

With Robert ruled out as John Doe, they narrowed their focus to the remaining brothers. They scrutinized the records for Edward and Patrick, searching for any signs of life or death beyond 1985.

After hours of research and analysis, they found that Edward O'Connor and Patrick O'Connor had both left behind traces of their existence after 1985. Edward had relocated to a different state too and had a digital footprint that spanned several years. Patrick, also, had records indicating that he was alive and well beyond the time of Doe's death. They all appeared to be buried in the family crypt in the Mt. Carmel cemetery.

The pieces of the puzzle were coming together, and the evidence was pointing to one conclusion. "Lilly, I think this means the only remaining option is Richard."

Lilly nodded, "You're right. The trail of evidence leads us to Richard O'Connor. He's the missing brother we've been searching for, and he's the most likely match for the John Doe in Desert Oasis."

Olivia and Lilly shared a moment of quiet reflection, knowing that their diligent work had brought them to the truth. Richard O'Connor, born in 1939, was the missing piece of the puzzle they had been seeking all along. Now they just had to verify that.

It was late in the day and instead of getting started on the towns provided by Agent Beck and having to stop, or what usually happens, pull an all-nighter, Olivia and Lilly left to do their favorite mind-clearing activity – watch a movie. Getting caught up in an unrelated story and not having the responsibility of figuring it all out – oh, and let's not forget popcorn, made it the perfect end to an almost-perfect day.

CHAPTER TWELVE

T he next morning, Olivia and Lilly sat in their office, surrounded by stacks of case files and photographs, and a map. They had reached a crucial turning point in their investigation, and an idea began to take shape.

They were researching the towns of Des Moines, Iowa, Sydney, Nebraska, and Salt Lake City provided by Postal Inspector Agent Beck. As they did, they realized that all of the towns were literally right adjacent to the Union Pacific Railroad Line that ran next to Jackrabbit Mountain.

Lilly broached the subject, "Okay, right now it appears that Richard traveled to towns right on the train line. No car was ever found in Nevada, and apparently, he specifically requested his mail to go to these different places, months apart. Did he really hop the rails?"

"I don't know of any other option, other than hitchhiking, do you?" Olivia asked. "The rail lines seem too convenient and remember what Officer Johnson of the Union Pacific Police told us? Apparently, it was common, especially for males, to use the railway as transportation."

"Not my idea of fun, Liv, but I hear you. And, Richard was found right off the rail line in Desert Oasis. The bigger question is did he plan to do this? And how are we going to verify what happened in those towns or what might have happened along the way, that might have contributed to Richard's demise? That's a heck of a lot of land to cover."

Olivia sighed and said, "Yes, I realize that. Did something happen in one of those towns? Did someone follow him? Did something bad happen to him or was he just the victim of bad luck or bad health?"

"I don't think we'll really know unless we speak to his family and retrace his steps," added Lilly.

"Okay, what about if we take a trip to some of the towns along the Union Pacific line? It could give us a better understanding of the places John Doe might have passed through and potentially lead us to more clues about his journey." Olivia suggested.

Lilly nodded, her eyes alight with curiosity. "Oh, wow, wouldn't that be awesome! We've been searching online, but there's something unique about experiencing these towns firsthand. It would allow us to connect with the people, immerse ourselves in the local history, and gain a deeper perspective. And, need I not forget I've always wanted to take the train cross country."

Olivia unfolded the map on her lap, her eyes scanning the list of stops. "Wow, look at all these towns we could visit. It's like a cross-country adventure. Chicago, Rockford, and Galena, Illinois; Dubuque, Waterloo, Des Moines, and Council Bluffs, Iowa; Omaha, Fremont, Grand Island North Platte, and Sidney, Nebraska; Cheyenne, Laramie, Rawlins, Rock Springs, Green River, and Evanston, Wyoming; Ogden and Salt Lake, Utah.

Olivia's excitement grew as she continued. "Think about it. We could visit towns like Cheyenne, Rawlins, and Rock Springs. These places were thriving hubs along the railroad back in the 1980s. There might be locals who still remember that time, who can share stories or provide insights into the lives of those who worked along the railroad. And, we

would definitely want to stop in Des Moines, Sidney and
Salt Lake."

Olivia's gaze lingered on the screen, taking in the estimated travel time and distance. "According to Amtrak, the
journey takes about 34 hours and 20 minutes, covering a
distance of approximately 1257 miles. It's quite a trek, but
it'll be worth it for the experience."

Lilly nodded enthusiastically. "And the best part is that
we'll have the opportunity to explore some of these towns
along the way. We can step off the train, stretch our legs,
and maybe even meet some interesting locals."

Olivia chuckled, imagining the adventures that awaited
them at each stop. "You always know how to find the most
unique and exciting ways to travel, Lilly. Taking the train
would definitely be an unforgettable journey."

Lilly beamed with pride. "Well, what can I say? I have a
knack for adding a little fun and spontaneity to our investigations. And this train ride is the perfect way to do it."

They were about to get serious about the train trip when
Lilly realized they had lost track of the time,

Olivia and Lilly eagerly logged into their Zoom call with
Chris Murphy, grandson of Jeannie Murphy, believed to

be the half-sister to the unidentified John Doe, Robert O'Connor. They were excited to speak with him and gather any information that could help them in their investigation.

The virtual meeting began, with Chris appearing on the screen. He had a warm smile and a curious look in his eyes, clearly intrigued by the connection to his family's past.

"Hi Chris, thank you so much for joining us today," Olivia greeted him warmly. "We really appreciate your willingness to talk about your family history."

Chris nodded, his voice tinged with curiosity. "Of course, happy to help. It's fascinating to learn about our roots and the stories that connect us."

Lilly began. "As I mentioned, we are Forensic Genetic Genealogists and we've been doing some research on the O'Connor family for a client of ours. We've come across your great-grandfather Edward O'Connor and his second wife Lydia Stevens as DNA matches. It looks like they had four boys together: Edward Jr., Robert, Patrick, and Richard. Do you have any knowledge of them?"

Chris paused, thinking for a moment. "Well, I knew about Edward Sr. because he was my great-grandfather. I don't have too many details really, because it's kind of bad blood in the family. From what I know, and you probably would be better off talking to my uncle Daniel, I guess Edward had a pretty good business here in Chicagoland. He and my great-grandmother Ann got divorced and he married Lydia and had a bunch of kids with her. That didn't go over well with my grandmother Jeannie. I guess she felt more attention was paid to the new family than the first one. Gram kinda resented her dad and I'm really sure what happened when he decided to step down from the business. I'm told she refused to take the helm, out of spite. She was really a stubborn lady. Gram didn't really talk about that side of the family. I always assumed the sons were involved in the family construction business."

Olivia and Lilly exchanged a knowing glance. This information aligned with what they had discovered so far. "That's interesting, and yes, families can be difficult," Olivia responded. "Do you know where the boys are now?"

"I would assume here in the city. Like I said, we never associated with them, at least I haven't been around that side of the family. Uncle Dan might be able to give you some better answers, but, I'll warn you, he's got dementia pretty bad. On second thought, I don't know how much help he would be." Chris suggested.

Lilly nodded in understanding. "We're trying to fill in the missing pieces for our client and will all of the family going back and forth, divorces, death, remarriage, it can make it kind of difficult. We really appreciate your help."

Chris smiled appreciatively. "I think it's great what you both are doing. It's important to understand where we come from and the lives our ancestors lived. I hope I might have helped someone, even if it's just a small piece of the puzzle. We did not have a big family and I'm always open to more!"

Olivia nodded, gratitude evident in her voice. "Every piece counts. Thank you, Chris. It means a lot that you took the time to share your family history with us. We'll share your information with our client and get back to you if we can if we have any new information."

Their next call later in the day was with Dorothy Burton the granddaughter of Lydia O'Connor's sister Eileen. They were excited to speak with her and gather any information that could shed light on the Stevens family history and their connection to the unidentified John Doe. But, because nothing was confirmed, once again they had to go in with a light touch only referencing a possible DNA connection to their client.

As the virtual meeting began, Dorothy appeared on the screen. She had a kind smile and a warm presence and seemed ready to share her memories about her family's past.

"Hi Dorothy, thank you so much for joining us today," Olivia greeted her. "We're really grateful for your being open to talking about your family and the connection to our client."

Dorothy smiled warmly. "Of course, I'm happy to help in any way I can. It's always interesting to learn more about our family roots and the stories that tie us together."

Lilly jumped in. "We're Forensic Genetic Genealogists and we have a client with DNA that seems to tie to your family, the Stevens', and the O'Connor line. We've been research-ing the Steven's family history, and we understand that your grandmother Eileen was Lydia's sister. Do you recall any stories or memories about Edward and Lydia and their sons?"

Dorothy was lost in thought for a moment. "Oh, my grandmother used to talk about her sister Lydia and the boys. Edward and Lydia did really well with their business, and they were always so kind to my grandmother. I remember her mentioning how they would do nice things for her, especially during the holidays."

Olivia and Lilly shared a look, intrigued by the mention of the successful business. "Wow, great to hear," Olivia said. "We've been trying to piece together the history of the family and it looks like they made some influential contributions to the Chicago skyline. Do you happen to know anything like that?"

Dorothy's expression turned slightly solemn. "I remember hearing that 'the boys', as my mom used to call them, eventually got involved in the business and took over from Edward. But things didn't go well, and they ended up losing it. My mom never said much about how or why it happened, but I do remember she mentioned that Richard, in particular, was deeply affected by it. If I remember correctly, Richard had to take over for a while but then he disappeared and was never heard from again."

Lilly nodded, absorbing the information. While she was attentive to the emotional component of what Dorothy had revealed, the investigator in her had to stay on track and get as much information as she could. "Wow, that's heartbreaking. I can't imagine someone just disappearing. What happened to him? Did the police get involved?"

Dorothy's gaze shifted, a mix of uncertainty and caution in her eyes. "To be honest, I'm not entirely sure. There were always rumors in our family that certain areas of Chicago during that time were, well, mobbed up. There was speculation, you know? And when it came to Richard's disappearance, there was always this question mark hanging over it."

Olivia looked up from her notes. "Do you mean to say that Richard might have been involved with some unsavory characters or caught up in something dangerous?"

Dorothy nodded slowly. "That's the story that went around. Some family members wondered if he took off on his own, while others believed he may have been taken off if you catch my drift. The truth is, the family simply didn't know. Fear held the family back from going to the police. They didn't want any trouble, and they weren't sure what had happened to Richard. So, they let sleeping dogs lie."

Lilly's expression mirrored the gravity of the situation. "It must have been incredibly difficult for your family, living with that uncertainty all these years. As we are researching the family, we'd love to provide assistance in helping answer that question for you if you are open to it."

Dorothy sighed, a mixture of relief and sadness in her voice. "Wow, that would be incredible. Thank you both for pursuing this. It means a lot to me and my family. Even if we never find out what truly happened, at least we'll know that someone cared enough to try."

Olivia nodded, offering reassurance. "We're committed to getting to the bottom of this, Dorothy. We'll let you know what we find, and please don't hesitate to reach out if you remember anything else that could be helpful."

As the Zoom call ended and Dorothy bid them farewell, Olivia and Lilly were left in a stunned silence. The weight of Dorothy's words hung heavily in the air, the realization sinking in that Richard's disappearance might have been far from voluntary. The possibility of organized crime involvement opened up a new and daunting chapter in their investigation, one that sent shivers down their spines.

Olivia broke the silence, her voice laced with a mixture of awe and concern. "Man, oh, man. Did you hear that? The mob? It's starting to make sense. The dismemberment, the fear that kept the family silent for so long. We may be dealing with something far bigger and more dangerous than we ever anticipated."

Lilly nodded, her mind racing with the implications of this revelation. "It adds a whole new dimension to the case. If Richard's disappearance was connected to organized crime, then we can't underestimate the level of power and influence involved. We need to tread carefully and be prepared for any challenges that come our way."

While excited at the newfound revelation, Olivia and Lilly understood that their investigation had taken a dark and dangerous turn. The path ahead could be treacherous, filled with more secrets, and the possible presence of organized crime. But armed with their expertise and unwavering commitment, they were ready to confront the truth and unveil the mysteries that had haunted the O'Connor family for far too long.

CHAPTER THIRTEEN

I t was rainy and cloudy outside as Olivia and Lilly settled into their chairs at the office, their faces etched with concern. The weather seemed to perfectly mirror their moods this morning. The events of the previous day, and the revelations from Dorothy, had left them restless and plagued with unsettling thoughts. It was evident on their faces that sleep had eluded them throughout the night, their minds consumed by the various possibilities of what could have happened to Richard.

Lilly let out a tired sigh, rubbing her temples. "I couldn't stop thinking about Richard. His disappearance and the potential involvement of organized crime. It kept replaying in my mind like a broken record, and every scenario seemed worse than the last."

Olivia nodded bleakly. "I know exactly what you mean. It's like a whirlwind of theories and conjectures spinning around in my head. Did he stumble upon something he shouldn't have? Was he forced to leave? The possibilities are haunting, and the weight of it all kept me awake."

They exchanged a knowing look. Today was a crucial day—the day they would fill in Chief Thompson about the new developments in the case. They needed to gather their thoughts, present their findings, and prepare to continue their work.

Lilly took a deep breath. "We can't let our restless nights slow us down, Olivia. We need to stay focused and push forward. Chief Thompson needs to know about Dorothy's revelations, about the potential involvement of organized crime. It's crucial for the investigation."

Olivia's eyes held unwavering resolve. "You're right. We need to be clear, concise, and persuasive when we present our findings, even if we don't like what we found. This is our chance to rally the resources and support necessary to dig further into the case."

Olivia, Lilly, and Chief Thompson gathered virtually over Zoom, the ladies' expressions reflecting a mixture of seriousness and determination. They had requested the video call, recognizing the gravity of the information they were about to share.

"Chief Thompson, thank you for taking the time to meet with us today," Olivia began, her voice composed yet filled with a sense of urgency. "We felt it was necessary to have this conversation over Zoom due to the nature of the information we've uncovered."

The Chief nodded. "Okay, Olivia. Let's get down to business. What have you found?"

Lilly jumped in, her voice steady but tinged with excitement. "Chief, based on our research and conversations with family members, we strongly believe that our John Doe is Richard O'Connor, born in Chicago in 1939. The timelines, DNA, documents and relatives statements align, pointing to Richard as the likely match."

Chief Thompson sat up straighter. "Richard O'Connor? One of the son's of Edward and Lydia O'Connor?"

Olivia nodded. "Yes. We have been able to establish a solid DNA connection between Edward's sons and the unidentified John Doe. We have spoken to a cousin, Dorothy, who states that one son, Richard went missing around the same time period in our case. However, there are some concerning aspects we need to address. The possibility of organized crime involvement has come up, and it may be related to Richard's disappearance."

Chief Thompson's brow furrowed, his expression growing serious. "Organized crime? Are you suggesting that Richard may have gotten involved with the wrong people?"

Lilly answered, her voice filled with concern. "It's a possibility, Chief." Lilly proceeded to recount Dorothy's narrative. "It's a crucial angle we need to explore further."

"And Chief, while this sounds ominous," Olivia mentioned, "We don't know that Richard was the victim of foul play or that he didn't just decide to take off on his own. Plus, we have no details and most of the family that would be able to tell us are mentally incapacitated or have passed away. Last but certainly not least, is that we have no formal cause of death. Richard could have succumbed to the elements for all we know."

Chief Thompson took a moment to process the information, his gaze shifting between Olivia and Lilly. "I see. This is indeed a significant development. We need to consider all possibilities and ensure we approach this investigation with the utmost caution."

Olivia continued, her voice steady. "Yes, I hear you. Before I forget Chief, we received a list of towns from the postal inspector, locations Richard had arranged for general delivery of his mail, from Chicago out to Desert Oasis. We believe these towns could hold key information or potential leads regarding Richard's whereabouts and the circumstances surrounding his disappearance. We're going to start focusing on those towns and what information might be available there."

Chief Thompson nodded, his expression thoughtful. "Very well. I appreciate the thoroughness of your investigation. It's clear we have a complex case on our hands. I can allocate additional resources and support to assist you in your search through those towns if need be."

"Thanks, Chief, that will be a big help to break through red tape and expedite the process." Olivia added, "One more thing since we're pretty confident of our identification, would you like us to prepare our report so you can review it for formal ID and coroner approval?"

"Yes, that would be great. Better to start that sooner than later. Email it over please when you have it." The Chief added.

After hanging up with the Chief, Olivia, and Lilly began to look deeper into the life of Richard O'Connor, attempting to retrace his steps documented by the General Delivery and unravel the enigma of his year-long journey on and off the rail line. Armed with the knowledge of the towns he had passed through along the Union Pacific line, they sought to understand the experiences that shaped his existence during that fateful year in 1982.

Recognizing the significance of local newspapers as a source of information, they reached out to the libraries, genealogical societies, and museums in each town, requesting access to any records or articles related to the time period shown on the general delivery schedule.

Armed with a trove of newspapers and articles, Olivia and Lilly began to comb through the faded digital pages, seeking fragments of truth that could shed light on Richard O'Connor's experiences. They hoped to uncover any traces of his existence, moments captured in ink that might reveal his encounters, struggles, or acts of kindness.

As they were doing so, across the country, Agent Beck, a seasoned investigator from the Postal Inspector's office, could hardly contain her excitement. She had made an extraordinary discovery during her requested inspection of the Desert Oasis post office. The "dead letters" section, typically containing forgotten and undeliverable mail, had yielded unexpected treasures this time. Among the items she found were actual letters for Richard O'Connor that had been saved all this time.

Agent Beck dialed Olivia's number, eager to share the remarkable find.

The phone rang a few times before Olivia picked up. "Agent Beck?" she answered.

"Hi Olivia, it's Luane!" She exclaimed, her voice filled with excitement.

"Hey, there! What's going on? You sound really pumped up," Olivia replied, picking up on Beck's enthusiasm.

Beck couldn't contain her excitement any longer. "You won't believe what was found at the Desert Oasis Post Office. Among the 'dead letters,' the Postmaster discovered THE actual letters addressed to Richard O'Connor!"

There was a moment of stunned silence on the other end of the line before Olivia could respond. "Wait, really? You found letters mailed to Richard O'Connor? Holy cow!"

Agent Beck couldn't help but grin. "Yes, I couldn't believe it myself. These letters have been sitting there all this time, preserved like a time capsule from the past."

Lilly, who had been listening in, piped up, "That's amazing! Do you know what's in the letters?"

"I haven't had a chance to read them in detail yet," Beck explained, "but I knew I had to tell you both right away. We have to be careful about privacy and all that but because we have a formal police investigation and we believe this could help identify your remains, we went ahead and opened and scanned them. I'll send them over first thing in email."

Olivia's excitement matched Beck's – about a 15 on a scale of 10. "Great idea! I can't wait to see what they say."

Agent Beck nodded enthusiastically, though they couldn't see her. "I knew you'd be excited too! I'll get them out now. Let me know when you've had a chance to review them."

Olivia and Lilly paced in eager anticipation as the printer finally spat out the scanned copies of the once-in-a-million find from the Postal Inspector's office. Clutching the sheets in their hands, they quickly made their way back to Olivia's desk, their curiosity bubbling over.

Olivia carefully laid out the documents on the desk, and the two women leaned in to examine the first one. It appeared to be a wage information document for tax purposes. They scrutinized the details, noting that it was from a company called Iowa Freight, based in Des Moines, Iowa. The fact that Richard O'Connor had tax forms from a company in Des Moines intrigued them.

Lilly's forehead wrinkled. "Iowa Freight in Des Moines? That's interesting. I wonder why he was receiving wage information from there."

Olivia nodded. "It could be a job he held, or maybe he had some financial ties to the company. It is one of the cities right on the rail line and one of the stops on the General Delivery timeline Agent Beck gave us."

Moving on to the next document, they saw it was another tax form, this time from a company called Able's in Sydney, Nebraska. Olivia noticed this form was also addressed to Richard O'Connor and was postmarked in January of 1983.

"Another tax form, but from a different company and location," Olivia remarked, her curiosity growing. "It seems like Richard had connections to multiple places."

Lilly agreed, "Yes, and Sydney is also on the train line, west of Des Moines, and a stop on the General Delivery list."

Before they could fully digest the information, their attention shifted to the last tax form, this time from Tell Oil in Salt Lake. Olivia's eyes widened as she noted the January 1983 postmark, similar to the others.

"Three different companies, three different locations," Olivia mused, "all linked to Richard O'Connor and his mail schedule."

Lilly pointed out, "We can cross-reference these companies, see if there are any connections or patterns that might shed light on his life."

Their excitement reached a new height as they turned their attention to the next documents. They appeared to be personal letters. Olivia carefully examined the first one, postmarked February 1, 1982, and noticed the return address from Chicago, sent by someone named Angela Edwards.

"A personal letter from Angela Patterson in Chicago," Olivia said. "I wonder what their relationship was."

Lilly looked thoughtful. "Well, we're about to find out, right?"

Olivia began to recite the first letter, dated January 1, 1982, addressed to 'Rich'. As she started to read, the emotions poured from the pages, and her heart went out to the woman who had penned these heartfelt words. Lilly leaned in, listening intently, captivated by the unfolding love story.

"So, in this Happy New Year's letter, Angela expresses how much she misses Richard," Olivia began, her voice soft and compassionate. "She speaks of their love and how she can't wait to be reunited with him once he's settled in a good location. It seems they were deeply connected before Richard left Chicago. She praises him for his dedication despite the hardships they faced during the recession, especially having to shut down the family business." Olivia continued. "She's proud of him for wanting to start a new life with her, embracing the opportunity to leave Chicago behind."

Lilly chimed in, "It appears Richard's pursuit of a better future was driven by his love for Angela and the desire to create a stable life for them together. But no mention of the mob or anything sinister."

"Right." Olivia posited. "Angela mentions how she's been following the news about trucking in Iowa, the decline in business, and the issues with the Union. I wonder if Richard first went to work there and was laid off. That could be the Iowa Freight."

Lilly added, "True. Then she says she's glad he was able to secure a good-paying job at the oil company in Salt Lake, which must have been a relief for both of them. Is that the Tell Oil? I'm sure he could have worn overalls at both the trucking company or the oil company, or both."

The letter seemed to be a blend of longing and excitement for the future. Olivia noted, "Angela admits things are still tough in Chicago, with continued layoffs, but she's hopeful for a fresh start with Richard. So we think this is Richard's plan all along, to get good work, a better opportunity and then send for Angela."

"I believe so." Lilly nodded in understanding, "It must have been hard for them to be apart during such challenging times, but it seems like Angela sees a glimmer of hope in the future they plan to build together."

Olivia chuckled softly, "It appears Angela is quite anxious for Richard to hurry up, despite knowing he's methodical. She just can't wait to be with him again."

Lilly smiled, "Love can be quite impatient at times, especially when you're eager to start a new chapter in your life."

Olivia set the letter down, a sense of connection to Richard and Angela forming as she contemplated Angela's words. "Okay, we agree it's evident that Richard and Angela's love is a driving force in his decision to seek better opportunities in a new location. No mention of threats, no one chasing after him, and nothing sinister. Their bond is strong, and I can imagine it has been challenging for them both."

Lilly nodded in agreement, "We have a glimpse into their personal lives now, and it's heartwarming to see how love has motivated Richard to keep pushing forward despite the hardships."

Olivia flipped to the second personal letter, dated March 15, 1982, also from Angela Edwards in Chicago, addressed to Richard O'Connor, also in Desert Oasis. As she read aloud, the tone of the letter took a different turn, leaving Olivia and Lilly intrigued yet concerned about the emotions behind Angela's words.

"What a difference a few months make. In this letter, Angela seems accusatory," Olivia began, her voice tinged with a mix of curiosity and concern. "She's questioning why Richard hasn't written to her and wonders if he has found someone else."

Lilly looked pensive and she sighed, nodding her head.

"It appears Angela is trying to be understanding and patient, but her worries are evident. She doesn't know how much longer she can hold on without any communication from Richard." Olivia said. "She urges him to be honest and just be straight with her about what's going on."

Lilly sighed softly, "It's clear that Angela is feeling anxious and hurt by the lack of communication. She's reaching out to him, seeking clarity and reassurance."

"Right but apparently not getting it. Angela says she's been telling herself that he's just busy with work and the move, but she can't shake the feeling of uncertainty." Olivia added.

Lilly nodded, "It must have been hard for her to be in the dark about Richard's whereabouts and his silence on their relationship."

Olivia's voice softened, "She told him that she loved him deeply and thought they had something special. She just wants to know the truth, no matter how difficult it may be. Who wouldn't want that?"

Lilly looked thoughtful, "It seemed like Angela was grappling with her emotions, torn between her love for Richard and her need for answers. Gosh, I think that we all have been in this place maybe a time or two."

Olivia looked at Lilly. "It's evident that Angela was hurting and in need of reassurance from Richard. She was trying to give him the benefit of the doubt, but the uncertainty was taking a toll on her."

Lilly nodded in understanding, "It's a challenging situation for both of them. Richard's silence may be unintentional, but it clearly affected Angela deeply."

Olivia sighed, "It's a reminder that behind every mystery, there are real people with real emotions. Angela's feelings were genuine, and we can't forget that."

Olivia and Lilly sat together, contemplating the significance of the letters and the timelines they revealed. The puzzle surrounding Richard O'Connor's disappearance seemed to grow more complex with each piece of information they uncovered.

Lilly broke the silence. "So, Richard's first employment was in 1982 in Des Moines, Iowa. His next employment was in Sydney, Nebraska in 1982, and his last known employment was in Salt Lake, and the tax form from Tell Oil is dated January 1983. Angela's letters are addressed to Richard via General Delivery in Desert Oasis."

Olivia paused, absorbing the details. "Right. He had already left Salt Lake by January 1983. But the troubling part is that he never responded to Angela's letter."

Lilly's eyes widened with realization. "Does that mean he was already deceased at that time? Could his lack of response be an indication of what happened to him?"

Olivia's expression mirrored Lilly's concern. "It's possible. If he were alive and well, one would expect him to reply, especially considering the emotional content of Angela's letter. But the fact that he didn't respond raises questions but can help us establish our timeline."

Lilly leaned back in her chair, deep in thought. "If Richard had passed away by January 1983, that would place his death sometime between his employment in Salt Lake sometime in 1982 and the date of the letter. But we still don't know how long he was in Desert Oasis before his body was found in March 1983."

Olivia agreed, "Exactly. We can't pinpoint the exact time of his death without more information about his activities and whereabouts during that period."

Lilly's eyes brightened as an idea struck her. "Maybe we should retrace his steps from Salt Lake to Desert Oasis. If we can find anyone who had contact with him or knew about his movements during that time, it might shed light on what happened."

Olivia nodded in agreement, "That's a good approach. We need to interview people who might have interacted with Richard during his journey from Salt Lake to Desert Oasis. They might have clues about his state of mind or any encounters he had along the way."

Lilly added, "And we should also look into the circum-stances surrounding his employment at Tell Oil. Was he content with the job? Did he have any issues that might have influenced his decision to leave?"

Olivia scribbled down some notes, "Right, we need to ex-plore every angle. Perhaps his employment history could give us more insight into his mindset and the events lead-ing up to his disappearance."

As they sat together, Olivia and Lilly realized that there was much more to uncover than just the facts of Richard O'Connor's disappearance. His personal relationships and the emotions tied to them were crucial pieces of the puzzle. They understood that they needed to handle the investiga-tion with sensitivity and empathy, as they were now deal-ing with not only the mystery of Richard's whereabouts but also the hearts of those who loved him.

CHAPTER FOURTEEN

O livia and Lilly, driven by their quest to unravel the mysteries surrounding Richard O'Connor's quest, had focused on the small towns along the Union Pacific rail lines. In one of the online archives, the story of the Anonymous Samaritan caught their attention, sparking their curiosity to learn more about the enigmatic man who had performed this hidden act of kindness in 1982.

In the town of Rock Springs, Wyoming the two women found a community with a rich history and a deep sense of solidarity. According to the reporter, the Thompson family, the recipients of the Anonymous Samaritan's goodwill in 1982, had been eager to share their story.

Now, over Zoom, with a glance into the Thompsons' living room, surrounded by faded family photographs, Olivia and Lilly listened intently as Bill Thompson, now a much older man, recounted the events of that fateful year. His voice carried a mix of gratitude and nostalgia as he painted a vivid picture of the struggles they had faced.

"It was a tough time for us," Bill began, his eyes filled with memories. "I had just lost my job at the coal mine, and my new wife and I were barely making ends meet. The future seemed uncertain, and we didn't know how we would provide for our children."

Olivia nodded, empathizing with the Thompsons' plight. "And that's when the Anonymous Samaritan entered your lives," she prompted, encouraging Bill to continue.

A smile graced Bill's face as he recalled the moment of their unexpected encounter. "I remember it like it was yesterday. We were sitting at our kitchen table, contemplating our next move, when there was a knock on the door. Standing before us was a man, worn and weary from his travels."

Lilly nodded, urging Bill on. "What did he say? How did he know about your situation?"

Bill chuckled softly. "He didn't say much. Just explained that he had heard about our family's struggles and wanted to help. He was from Chicago, passing through town, hopping freight trains, and had managed to find some temporary work on a nearby farm. With the little money he earned, he bought us groceries and supplies, enough to sustain us for weeks."

Olivia couldn't help but feel a profound sense of admiration for the Anonymous Samaritan who they believed to be Richard O'Connor. "He must have known what it was like to struggle, to face uncertainty. Yet, he selflessly extended a helping hand."

Bill nodded, his eyes glistening with gratitude. "That's what struck me the most. Here was a man with his own hardships, yet he didn't hesitate to help us. We never learned his name, but we called him the 'Anonymous Samaritan' because that's what he was to us—a guardian angel in our time of need. I just wish I had a chance to repay him or follow up with him, to let him know how much he meant to us and our survival."

The conversation continued with the Thompson family, as stories of the town's resilience and the kindness of its residents unfolded. Olivia and Lilly discovered that the impact of the Anonymous Samaritan's act of kindness went far beyond the Thompsons' household. It had become somewhat of a legend like today's 'pay it forward' campaigns, whispered from one generation to the next, reminding the community of the power of compassion and selflessness.

Olivia and Lilly, while unable to reveal the full details of the story, let Bill and his family know they were doing research on the O'Connor family and believed their stranger might have been one of the sons. They showed a graduation photo and one where Richard was a groomsman and Bill's eyes lit up. "Well, I'll be damned. It's got to be him. I'll never forget that face." Bill said as he leaned into the computer screen. "Would you please, if you speak to him, let him know what he meant to us and the town."

Olivia and Lilly promised they would.

Signing off the call, Olivia and Lilly carried with them not only the details of their investigation but also the profound impact of the Anonymous Samaritan's story. They recognized the significance of this hidden good deed, not only in unraveling the enigma of Richard O'Connor's identity but also in reminding them of the innate goodness that can exist even in the face of adversity.

As they turned back to their work, Olivia and Lilly couldn't help but wonder how many more stories of compassion and generosity lay hidden in the annals of Richard O'Connor's life. Their determination to uncover his identity burned brighter than ever, fueled by the belief that the man they sought was more than just a nameless face—he was a complex tapestry of experiences, connections, and moments of grace.

Searching through the archives, they could find no further mention of Richard O'Connor or surprising good deeds in any of the small towns. Too, they did not find mention of Richard in Desert Oasis or thankfully, any mob-related events near or around that time.

With Richard identified and his story mostly told, it was time to sum it up for the Chief and sign off the investigation.

Olivia spent the next few days writing the final report while Lilly finished up with Victoria and Jennifer and the myriad of ever-increasing new clients. When it was done, she emailed it to Chief Thompson and scheduled a time for the three of them to go over any questions.

A few days later, the three of them were on the phone, and Chief Thompson had the M.E. Dr. Peterson in his office.

Chief Thompson began, "First of all ladies, I can't begin to tell you how impressed I was with your investigation and your detailed report. Dr. Peterson feels he can clear the case and make a positive identification but I thought we'd share one last get-together in case any questions come to mind. I'll summarize and please stop me if I misstate anything."

"Sure Chief, the floor's all yours," Olivia said.

"Alright, to recount. We found the unidentified male in 1983 at the base of Jackrabbit Mountain. We have no official cause of death as we only had skeletal remains and not much of them. Though much research was done on the personal items found with the Doe, whom we are now officially referring to as Richard O'Connor, they were not definitive. In contacting the Postal Inspector's office, they ruled out any potential employee with the last name ending in '...iffe' and the one they did have was hired after Richard's date of death. This name, which could be tied to the partial monogram, was believed to be for a sample, and not a real person. The traveling salesman, who might have had this clothing, a guy by the name of Tom, doesn't show up in our DNA."

Olivia and Lilly added, "Mmm, hmmm."

The Chief continued, "Speaking of DNA, the results show that our Doe is one of four O'Connor sons from Chicago. In researching those names, the Postal Inspector found unclaimed mail in the name of Richard O'Connor, in the 1982 and 1983 time period. Further, they were able to track the locations back as originating in Chicago, where Richard O'Connor, born in 1939, hails from."

"Yes, Chief," Olivia added.

"Okay," he continued, "You were able to speak to relatives of the O'Connors and found that three of the sons appeared to have lived, and died, after 1983. Richard, after losing the family business around 1982, took off and was never heard from again. Though, in a weird break of luck, the Desert Oasis post office found actual mail addressed to our Richard and we reviewed those. Three are from former employers which track to his purported train trip across the U.S. and two were confirming stories from what appears to be his girlfriend Angela Edwards. She confirms his trip out from Chicago and seems to confirm his want of a new start. Despite the times in Chicago and the condition of the body, she makes no mention of fear or escape or anything related to organized crime."

Lilly agreed, "Yes, sir."

"Okay, so thankfully no mob hit and amazingly we have a good deed done in Rock Springs. The old guy tells the story of the good soul from Chicago who helped him out back then and identifies Richard from two photos found online, one of which was a family wedding. You spoke to Dorothy, a cousin, who said that Richard disappeared without a trace after losing the business and was not heard from again. So, it all adds up, right?"

"Perfectly, sir." said Olivia, "And I've also found two more things that tie it up nicely. We were able to match Richard's social on the death master file with the tax forms we had from the dead letter file. And, while it could be any one of the brothers, all with no offspring, Lilly and I made a trip to the family plot at Mt. Carmel here in Chicago and took a look at the headstones, cemetery, and funeral home paper-work and the death certificates which only leave Richard outstanding. I can send those over as attachments to the original report."

"Well, I think that's more than we have in a lot of cases, ladies. What say you Doc?" The Chief asked.

Dr. Peterson answered. "I'm good here. I can make the identification but I'll have to leave the death undetermined. I'm not sure we will ever know but his family will have closure of sorts, and I'll release the body so he can have a proper burial as they see fit."

"Speaking of family," said Olivia, "Will you need us to reach out or will your office follow up with notifications?"

"You've done so much already, we can take it from here." The Chief answered. "I hope we won't have the unfortunate instances to reach out to you again but if we do, I know you will make it an open and shut case. It's really extraordinary what you do and the police are thankful to have it. Again, much appreciated, and I hope you can spend some fun time focused on the living."

The ladies thanked the Chief and hung up. Olivia opened her email and quickly forwarded the information on the social security number and the cemetery details. She spun around and with a big smile on her face said to Lilly, "I don't know about you, but I've got a hottie and a plane waiting for me. While you always know where to find me, for the next few days, please don't."

CHAPTER FIFTEEN

The next week, Olivia and Lilly stood together in the conference room, a map of the United States still on the wall before them. The idea of taking a train trip cross country to follow Richard's moves had been enticing, but now that they had solved the mystery and knew all about him, it was in the past, or was it?

Lilly tapped her finger on the map. "You know, Olivia, I think it's wonderful that we wanted to take this train trip to retrace Richard's steps. It would have been like following his journey and understanding his life better."

Olivia nodded in agreement, a thoughtful expression on her face. " It was a great idea, and I'm sure it would have given us even more insight into his experiences and the places he went."

"But now that we've uncovered all the details about Richard's life," Lilly continued, "the mystery is no longer clouding our understanding of him. We know where he lived, worked, and the impact he had on others. We can mostly see the full picture of his life."

Olivia smiled, "You're right. With the mystery solved, the train trip would be more of a celebration of his life rather than a quest for answers. It would be a journey to honor his memory and the journey he took."

Lilly's eyes lit up with enthusiasm, "Exactly! We can plan it for the future as a tribute to Richard and all the lives we touch through our work. A journey of exploration and appreciation for the people we seek to understand."

Olivia grabbed a pen and circled the map around some of the places Richard had lived and worked. "I love that idea. We can visit these places, learn more about the communities he was a part of, and maybe even meet some of the people he knew."

Lilly added, "And without the cloud of loss hovering over us, we can fully immerse ourselves in the experience. It will be a journey of discovery and connection."

The excitement in the room grew as they started brainstorming potential stops along the train route. They imagined the sights they would see, the stories they would hear, and the memories they would create.

Olivia laughed, "I can already picture us, riding the train, with notebooks in hand, jotting down all the interesting things we learn about the places Richard called home."

Lilly chimed in, "And of course, we'd take loads of pictures to capture the essence of each destination and the spirit of our adventure."

As they continued to discuss their future train trip, the weight of the recent investigation lifted, leaving them feeling uplifted and inspired. They knew that their work as investigators was not just about solving mysteries; it was about understanding lives, connecting with people's stories, and providing closure to those who sought answers.

With renewed enthusiasm, they decided to take some time to plan their future train journey. They knew that when the time came, it would be a journey filled with apprecia-

tion and a celebration of life—a tribute to Richard and all
the other lives they would touch along the way.

That Saturday was a quiet one for Olivia. She awoke on a
mission, albeit a different one.

She drove through the gates at the Mt. Carmel cemetery
and found the crypt of the O'Connor family. She took
some flowers and took a few minutes to have a conversation with Edward and Lydia, and Richard's brothers,
telling them about his adventures and how he meant so
much to not only Angela but the Thompsons, the Rock
Springs community, and uniquely to her. She thanked
them for raising a great son and told them he would be
with them soon.

Olivia then headed a few manicured lots over again giving
thanks. This time to her grandfather, who also was laid to
rest there. While she had not unraveled all of his story yet,
she thanked him for raising a great son, said she was grateful for him, and even the DNA drama because it allowed

her to do this great work. Nothing by happenstance she said to herself shaking her head.

As she headed back to her car, she breathed in the fresh air and all the possibilities and drove off in search of their next adventure.

Afterword

Thank you for purchasing and reading this book. It is important to me in so many ways.

More importantly, it's important to the **over 14,400 unidentified humans** that remain in morgues and unmarked graves across the United States.

These are people's mothers, fathers, sisters, brothers, and children.

They may be victims of crimes or just left this earth and remain nameless.

I aim to change that.

It's scary to write, publish and put it all out there but I couldn't go on without doing *something* for these poor people.

I created these books to raise awareness of these cases – this book was inspired by one.

The Unknown Humans Remain podcast does exist, another avenue to spread the word.

https://youtu.be/p5ebI_r-CKQ

For more information and to join us in the initiative, please register for our newsletter:

https://dashboard.mailerlite.com/forms/445024/90623 140122593073/share

Last but not least, please consider leaving a helpful review on Amazon letting me know what you thought of the book.

Thank you!

Christine

First In The Series

#1 Best Seller On Amazon

Meet Olivia and Lilly!

Get Your Copy Now

Dead bodies, dark secrets, DNA and genetic genealogy. Can Olivia identify Jane Doe and her killer without losing herself in the process?

In Concrete Clues Olivia and Lily embark on a thrilling journey of discovery, utilizing the cutting-edge technique of genetic genealogy to solve the baffling mystery surrounding a nameless Jane Doe. As they delve into the depths of her past, they uncover a web of lies, deception, and long-kept secrets.

https://www.amazon.com/dp/B0C7SV5Y7C

Pony Tale Publishing

Printed in Great Britain
by Amazon